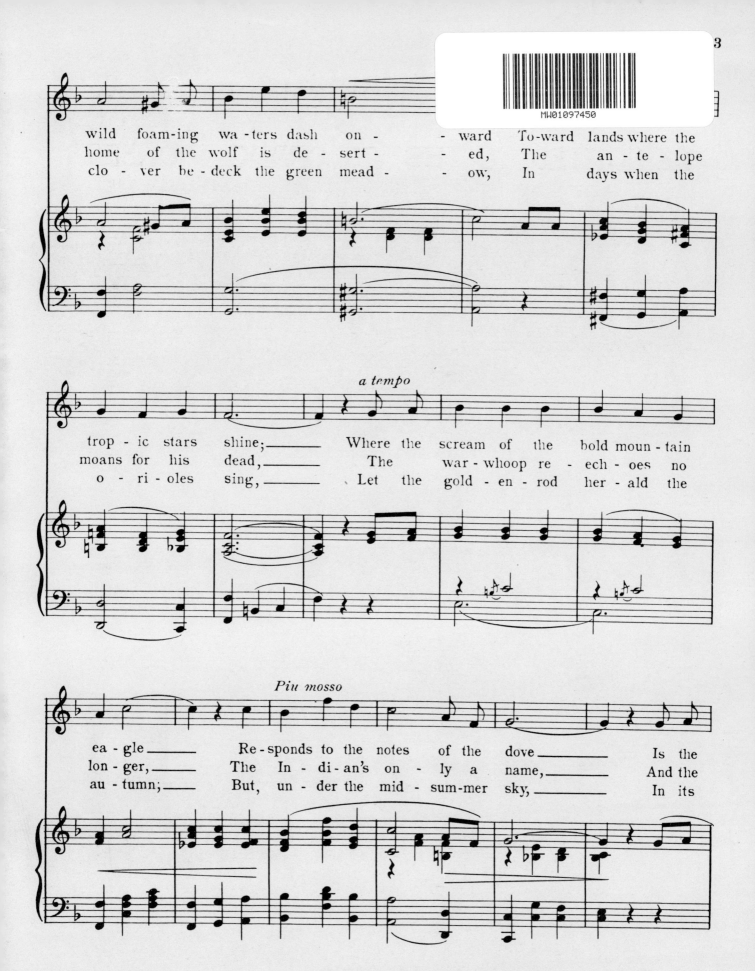

TRAILS Among the COLUMBINE

A Colorado High Country Anthology

1832

SUNDANCE Books

Editor's Preface

This volume marks the beginning of a new series of Sundance books. Western history and railroad history have been our particular areas of interest, with Colorado narrow-gauge our emphasis. Through the years we have discovered something which really came as no surprise: many readers with a serious interest in western history and the history of Colorado's mountain railroads find the setting in which the rails were laid as fascinating to experience and read about as the railroads and iron horses which drew them there in the first place. The temperament which finds solace (and excitement) in contemplation of steam engines winding through the mountains, which is filled with joy in the act of reading about the age of steam in the Rockies, often finds the same pleasure in tales of high country adventure, in the viewing of photographs which depict the rugged mountains and lush valleys through which the rails were laid, and in stories of wilderness and the creatures who abide there. We are, for I must include myself in this group, romantics. We are deeply moved by our memories and knowledge of what once was, and we are deeply moved by the best of what still is. It is by this temperament we at Sundance have been motivated in the past, and it is with the same spirit we move into this new endeavor.

Those readers who have been with us for a while will immediately recognize the series' title as having come from our scenic calendar series, "Trails Among the Columbine." In that group of calendars we attempted to depict, visually, the beauty of the high country. Many of our readers asked for more, and in attempting to satisfy our readers we found the calendar format to be too limiting. Twelve photographs and captions a year would never be enough. The calendar evolved into an idea for a book, and the book into a series of books.

In the current volume we have brought together a collection of writing, photography and illustration with fairly broad thematic content. We go from early Colorado history, to adventures in her new wilderness areas, with stops along the way in rebuilding history, recreation and travel. There is serious history here, as well as simple play. But all of it is unified by the same backdrop: the mountains of Colorado.

It is our hope that our readers will find a great deal of pleasure in this series; those of us who have had a part in putting it together have certainly enjoyed the process. It is also our hope that the series will continue to grow and provide pleasure to its readers for many years to come.

Steven J. Meyers, Editor

FRONT COVER: The Vermillion Peaks of the San Juan Mountains in southwestern Colorado tower above the Lizard Head Pass road near the town of Ophir.

Dell A. McCoy Photograph

BACK COVER: Blazing Star (Liatris punctata) spends the spring and summer as a nondescript, scraggly weed. In the late fall it explodes into bloom, greeting winter with a blaze of color. This one was photographed in the foothills west of Denver.

Robert W. McLeod Photograph

Trails Among The Columbine
A Colorado High Country Anthology

SUNDANCE PUBLICATIONS *Limited*
250 Broadway, Denver, Colorado 80203

Published by
Sundance Publications, Ltd., Denver, Colorado

Graphical Presentation and Printing by
Sundance Publications, Ltd., Denver, Colorado

Binding by
Hawley Bookbinding Co., Denver, Colorado

Typesetting by
The Silverton Standard and The Miner
Silverton, Colorado

Editor - Steven J. Meyers
Production Manager - Dell A. McCoy
Director of Photography - Steven J. Meyers
Graphic/Technical Production - Ernest Simkins

ISBN 0-913582-37-9

TABLE OF CONTENTS

Colorado Columbine

The Colorado Blue Columbine was adopted the official state flower of Colorado in 1899. It belongs to the Ranunculus or buttercup family. The lovely, long-spurred, nodding blossoms are Colorado sky blue with a snow white cup reminiscent of the champagne powder on the state's ski slopes. A profusion of yellow anthers recalls Colorado's gold rush days. In their natural state, Columbines are found in moist, shady places from the lower foothills to just above timberline, but they seem to be most beautiful in aspen groves around 8,000 feet in elevation. This hardy cluster was photographed catching the late afternoon sun above Silverton, Colorado.

Bill Wunsch Photograph

Winter fishing on the
Roaring Fork offers many
rewards, solitude being,
perhaps, the greatest.

The

Colorado Highway 82 never strays far from the rippling course of the Roaring Fork River as the road climbs steadily uphill from Glenwood Springs to Aspen. Most of the traffic in wintertime, when snow blankets the ranch valleys and puts white crowns on majestic Mt. Sopris and the jagged Maroon Bells, is ski-season traffic.

The foreign cars, vans and four-wheel drives bristle with ski racks. The drivers and passengers are headed toward one of the Aspen area's four ski mountains, or leaving one of those mountains.

Occasionally, a motorist will do a double-take, glancing down into the blue-green vein of the river in all that white, to see—yes, his eyes aren't deceiving him—a fly fisherman standing knee-deep in the flow.

He wonders: Is the man mad? A non-skier suffering from a terminal case of cabin fever? It isn't *fishing* season, is it?

Indeed it is. It is what some Colorado anglers think of as the "Solitude Season," or the "Frostbite Season." But fishing is definitely available in the austere winter beauty of the Roaring Fork Valley. For some years, a very small number of fishermen had it to themselves, this fishing in solitude, but word has gotten around. There is still no danger of fishing in a crowd, but the notion of winter fishing in the Colorado mountains is no longer considered eccentric.

On the Roaring Fork and its tributary, the Frying Pan River, fishing can be as good, if slightly more challenging, in the dead of winter as in the bloom of summer.

The Fork and the Pan. Culinary terms, perhaps, if your tastes run to exceptional angling for rainbow trout, brown trout and mountain whitefish.

The Roaring Fork Valley has a rich history of discovery. Fishing is part of it.

Before the white man came, the Ute Indians discovered the medicinal qualities of the hot mineral springs that gushed forth near the confluence of the Colorado River (first known as the Grand River) and the Roaring Fork.

In 1879, prospectors who journeyed over the pass from Leadville discovered the silver that was to create the mining boom-town of Aspen.

In the 1890s, the rest of the country discovered the therapeutic attractions of Glenwood Springs as a health spa.

In the 1940s, a few enterprising men discovered and began to develop the tremendous skiing potential of Aspen's Ajax Mountain. It marked the rebirth of Aspen, the burned-out mining town, as a world-famed ski mecca.

Precisely when modern-era fishermen discovered that trout in the Roaring Fork and Frying Pan could be caught as readily in winter as in spring or summer is not recorded, but it had to be sometime after 1962. That was the first year that the Colorado Wildlife Commission authorized a year-round trout season in the state. Anglers no longer had to wait for the spring, opening-day rush.

My own discovery of winter fishing on the Roaring Fork came one snowy day as I drove back toward Glenwood Springs after some newspaper coverage of an Aspen ski race. I did the old double-take, as I spotted three wader-clad fly fishermen diligently casting into a deep run downstream from Basalt.

One of those men, as I found out when I parked the car and walked over, was Chuck Fothergill of Aspen.

He was putting the finishing touches to a nice job of hooking, playing and landing a 17-inch brown trout.

Fothergill graciously took the time to inform me that he and his partners had caught and released some three dozen trout in that one run. The secret to this staggering revelation was a fly-fishing technique known as nymphing. It has nothing to do with apres-ski orgies, but rather with a deadly way of using an artificial fly which imitates the immature aquatic insects found on or near the stream bottom.

If anybody deserves the lion's share of the credit for telling Colorado anglers of the joys of nymphing in wintertime, it is Chuck Fothergill. As it turned out, we fished many times together over the next several years, as he showed me the tricks of his dead-drift, floating-fly-line method of nymph fishing.

There are variations of this technique which are as sophisticated as anything in fishing. But the basic tackle and tactics are simple:

A long (8 to 9-foot) fly rod. A floating fly line. A long (12 to 14-foot) tapered monofilament leader. A nymph fly on the end of the leader. (It could be any one of a fistful of effective patterns—the gold-ribbed Hare's Ear, the Renegade, the Golden Stonefly, the Colorado Caddis, the Pheasant Tail, the Brown

Solitude Season

by Bob Saile

The stark beauty of winter adds a new dimension to the fisherman's experience.

Patience is rewarded. The nymph fishing techniques often used on the Roaring Fork in winter result in many hooked fish, like this beautiful rainbow.

Although not as eagerly sought as its distant cousin, the trout, mountain whitefish like these provide excellent sport. They move willingly to the fly or lure even on the coldest days.

Hackle Peacock, to name some.) Finally, a split shot or wrap-around lead weight attached to the leader, about 18 inches above the fly, to sink the fly deep.

The fisherman casts, flings or slings (with weight on the leader, the cast tends to be somewhat less than graceful) the rig in a mostly *upstream* direction, so as to give the nymph time to sink before it drifts back toward him. He lets it be carried by the bottom current, just as a real-live insect would be carried if it had been shaken loose from a rock.

The fly and the leader are down, but the fly line is up—floating high on the surface. It acts as a bobber, or strike indicator. The nymph fisherman knows that if the end of that floating fly line pauses, stops, hesitates, twitches, backs up, jerks or does anything but float along at the pace of the current, he must set the hook! Sometimes, the fly has merely snagged on bottom. But other times, a fish has waylaid the nymph, and the angler is blessed with the grandest of angling sensations: The throb, up through line and rod, of a still unseen fish, deep in the river.

On either the Fork or the Pan, the fish is likely to be a rainbow or brown trout. But on the Fork particularly, it may be a whitefish, a sort of distant cousin of the trout that looks like a cross between the beauty of a grayling and the ugliness of a sucker.

A few years ago, the Colorado Division of Wildlife hauled electro-shocking equipment down the Roaring Fork between Basalt and Carbondale, stunning the fish to see how many were there. The good news, when they had tallied their impressive figures, was that in places, the river harbored up to 7,000 fish per mile!

Alas, the bad news was that the bulk of them were whitefish.

To most fishermen, the whitefish is less desirable than trout, because of its homely countenance, less than spectacular fight and bone-ridden, flaky flesh. But the whitefish is truly winter's child, almost always willing, even on the coldest days.

Whitefish of four pounds or more have turned up on the Roaring Fork over the years. In terms of whitefish, this makes the Fork a river of giants. The division of wildlife not long ago recorded a 5-pound, 2-ounce specimen caught by an Aspen angler. If this weight was accurate, it surpassed the still-listed world record by two ounces. But it apparently was not submitted for official world-record recognition.

The electro-survey statistics triggered some fast shuffling of the creel limits on the Roaring Fork. Most of the river was placed under a very conservative trout limit of one rainbow and one brown.

Meanwhile, the limit on whitefish was totally removed, raising visions of fishermen with large freezers and appetites to match hauling home truckloads of whitefish.

But it hasn't happened, and never will. Most fishermen come to the Roaring Fork in winter to satisfy not their larders, but their psyches. Most of them seek trout, and the new regulations on both the Fork and the Pan promise to maintain trout populations at a level approaching the "good old days," whenever *that* was.

Winter fishing is an adventure in a meteorological as well as an ichthyological sense. A drive over Vail Pass from Denver may border on a life-threatening experience, as icy pavement and sheets of falling snow inspire white-knuckle grips on the steering wheel.

But once safe in Glenwood Springs, an angler may seek the soothing panacea of a hot tub or a vapor cave or a dip in the world's largest outdoor, hot-water (92 degrees) swimming pool, at the Hot Springs Lodge. Or, if he likes local color, he may want to imbibe a bit at the old Doc Holliday Tavern on Grand Avenue, tipping one in memory of the tubercular gunfighter who is buried high on a rocky hillside overlooking the town. He may carve into a steak or gnaw on barbecued ribs at the Buffalo Valley Inn, or if particularly energetic, continue up the highway to Aspen, there to dance the evening hours away in an after-ski night club. Fortified by a few hours of sleep in a motel, he may arise to find that the clouds of the night before have become a sky of purest blue.

Such was the February morning that greeted Leonard Schmelz and me after a drive up from Denver the night before. The sky was blue and so was the thermometer, at a chilling 10 degrees above zero.

After breakfast, we drove up the valley, deciding to continue on to the Frying Pan River. The Roaring Fork was carrying thin chunks of floating slush ice, a condition which can occur on very cold mornings. We knew the ice would be gone by noon, but we wanted to begin fishing before then.

The Frying Pan, its flows warmed by the deep releases from Ruedi Dam, 15 miles upstream from Basalt, seldom has ice. It did not carry any this day.

By 10 a.m., the sun was warm on our goose-down jackets. Perhaps this was what encouraged us to fish not with fly rods, but with spinning tackle and lures, I don't recall. But I do know that it is more difficult to convince a cold-weather, slow-metabolism trout to chase a moving lure than it is to induce him to accept a slowly drifting nymph fly. We tied on Rooster Tail spinners anyway, fishing them on four-pound-test line and ultra-light rods and reels.

Amazingly, the trout of the Frying Pan loved it that February morning, as we cast toward the undercut banks in the Seven Castles area, where red-rock outcrops rise up like primitive battlements on some medieval fortification.

By 2 p.m., with the temperature having scaled the

Bob Saile Photograph

A friend's hookup can be as exciting as your own, especially when drifting nymphs. Is it a snag, or a fish? Only a lift of the rod tip, and the resulting throbbing response will tell you for certain. For every fish there are many false alarms, but when a fish is hooked ...

heights from near zero to the mid-40s in less than six hours, we had caught several nice browns and rainbows.

I was casting my spinner when it dawned on me, standing in a long, riffled run along the base of a basalt cliff, that I hadn't had a strike in several minutes. Something was wrong. Then I heard a splash. Then I *saw* a splash. No, something was *right*. Trout and the insects they feed on cannot read a calendar. These Frying Pan trout were rising to a hatch of tiny, bluish-gray mayflies!

It is still the earliest date I can remember seeing a mayfly hatch on any river in Colorado. But dry-fly fishing in winter on the Frying Pan is not all that uncommon, even if the mayflies aren't out. There is also a minuscule, grayish-black insect known as a midge (some fishermen call them "no-seeums") and they hatch year-round.

I do not move fast in chest waders through foot-deep snow, but I did a fair imitation of a sprint on the way back to the parked vehicle to retrieve a fly rod. The No. 18 size Blue Quill dry fly I chose was just what the doctor—and the trout—ordered. They sipped it under time after time, there in that sparkling, sun-splashed run in a snowy canyon carved by a river named for a cooking utensil.

These days, the Frying Pan is making a comeback after a few down years caused by increased, year-round fishing pressure. It, too, is under very conservative regulations—one fish of each species. This is not a river for the meat-hungry, but it is a mountain stream where a fisherman has a chance to catch a 6-pound brown or rainbow, as Joe Butler, a friend of mine did (he caught a rainbow of that size on a nymph) one recent January day.

No, skiing is not the only game in town, or in the Roaring Fork Valley, when winter puts a bear hug on the landscape. Each sport beckons and it is even possible to do both in one day. The big difference between the two is that while you may find a crowd, and long lift lines, on the ski mountain, you'll find solitude, or at least, minimal competition, on the trout stream.

Glenwood Springs, Aspen, Basalt, Carbondale. Names to be filed away in the back of any angler's mind, to be brought forth on winter days when the itch is strong to use a fishing rod. Interestingly, Glenwood Springs was originally called Defiance. The name derived from the Defiance Town & Land Co., which founded the town in 1882.

The name is gone, but in the Roaring Fork Valley, the defiance lives on—a defiance of the elements and the calendar, a slap in the face of Old Man Winter for those who take their fishing with a dash of solitude.

Ron Ruhoff Photograph

Colorado's Cross Of Snow

by Ron Ruhoff

A group of riders view 14005 foot Mount of the Holy Cross from the stone shelter on Notch Mountain.

Ron Ruhoff Photograph

On August 23, 1873, William H. Jackson, often called the "Pioneer Photographer of the West," reached the summit of a peak in the Sawatch Range and stood transfixed by what he saw. Before him, on the side of a huge mountain, was a perfect cross of snow complete with the figure of a kneeling woman at its side. He had at last found what he was after: the legendary Mount of the Holy Cross.

Jackson, heading the photographic division of the U.S. Hayden Geological Survey in Colorado, had heard many stories about the mountain with the snowy cross, but even those who claimed to have seen it from a distance could not tell him how to get there. When the survey party reached Tennessee Pass, it continued north through Eagle River Canyon to a point near the present-day town of Minturn. They then turned west, and, with much difficulty due to the rough terrain, followed what is now called Cross Creek Canyon. After camping overnight, Jackson ascended a nearby peak to try to get a better view of the surrounding area. The morning was foggy and visibility was near zero when he reached the summit of the mountain. While standing there, a breeze came up which swirled and then parted the clouds before him. Suddenly there was a breathtaking view of the great cross itself. The weather allowed only that one brief glimpse of the Mount of the Holy Cross that day, but Jackson knew he was at last on the right spot for a photograph.

The next day dawned clear, and Jackson set out with his bulky 11x14 wet plate camera, darkroom tent for development of plates on the spot and companions to help carry the equipment. The first, and probably the best, photographs ever taken of the mountain were made that day. Jackson made those exposures from the top of 13,734-foot Notch Mountain, which, even today, is the only spot allowing a full view of the 600 by 1,500 foot cross of snow.

As the years passed, Jackson's famous photographs made Notch Mountain and its wonderful view a very popular place to visit. On May 11, 1929, President Herbert Hoover proclaimed Mount of the Holy Cross a National Monument (the area in which it was located had been designated the Holy Cross National Forest by President Theodore Roosevelt in 1905). Shortly after President Hoover's proclamation, a trail was cut to the crest of Notch Mountain and a stone shelter cabin built. Many annual pilgrimages have been made to this cabin.

By 1951 rockslides and erosion had partially obliterated the right-hand arm of the cross. Interest in the mountain waned and the Holy Cross National Monument designation was dropped, the area becoming part of the White River National Forest.

In 1957 I purchased the book *Quest of the Snowy Cross* by Clarence Jackson, son of the pioneer photographer. This excellent little book (now out of print, but available in the Denver Public Library Western History collection) tells how the "Picture Maker of the Old West" first located and photographed the cross. After reading this fascinating story, I decided to climb Notch Mountain to see for myself just what the cross did look like.

On the morning of June 22, 1958, I left Halfmoon Campground, where I had camped overnight, and followed the Notch Mountain Trail to the shelter cabin. The Cross was a wonderful sight and seemed in remarkably good condition despite the reports of its destruction. My location provided a rather distorted view of the mountain and I realized that this was not the exact spot from which the Jackson photo had been taken. The shelter cabin is actually located in a saddle some distance south of the actual summit of Notch, where Jackson had been. Since the jagged notch, for which the mountain was named, separates the cabin from the summit, I could not get there quickly enough for pictures that day. I decided to return the following weekend, and did so with my friend Kenneth Barrow.

This time we took the right-hand trail from Halfmoon camp and headed for the actual summit via Halfmoon Pass. While climbing along the north ridge of Notch, Mount of the Holy Cross began to show itself in a more familiar outline. I had Clarence Jackson's little book with me, as I had on the first climb, and was comparing my angle of view with its illustrations. Some distance below the summit I noticed a large boulder which somehow looked very familiar. I pulled the book from my pack and looked through the pictures. Sure enough, there was the very same boulder, with a very young Clarence standing atop it, and the Mount of the Holy Cross in the background. This was a picture his father had taken on August 23, 1893, while on a 20th anniversary expedition to Notch Mountain. Clarence was then 17 years old. I promptly posed Ken on the rock in the same manner and duplicated the photo. Ken and I then continued on to the summit. Once there, it became obvious that we were at last on the exact spot where Jackson had made the first photo of the cross. The snow in the crevices which form the cross was absolutely perfect even though we had arrived to photograph two months earlier in the year than Jackson had! The right-hand arm of the cross was partially gone, but little imagination was needed to make it complete.

I showed the pictures I had taken to Clarence Jackson, who lived in a small hotel room in Denver until his death at the age of 85 in 1961. He said it was "utterly beyond him" how we could have found that rock on which he had perched 65 years earlier.

In 1962, Edwin M. Yeager of Evanston, Illinois, heard of our climb and became very interested. He had been to the Notch Mountain shelter cabin in June of that year and had also realized that he was in the wrong place to see the "Jackson Boulder," and to properly view the Mount of the Holy Cross. Yeager had brought a bronze plaque with him which commemorated both Clarence S. and William H. Jackson and had hoped to mount it on their boulder. When he reached the shelter and found it to be the wrong location, he left the plaque there, planning to return the following year to mount it.

Since Yeager was unable to return to Colorado in 1963, I went to the shelter cabin myself in June of that year with my friend Rex Myers of Denver. We arrived there late in the afternoon and were chased inside by an electrical storm. We found the plaque where Edwin had left it, and after taking a few pictures of the cross, descended back to Halfmoon Campground, carrying the plaque with us.

The following week I returned to Notch, this time with another friend, Jack L. Morison. We proceeded to the "Jackson Boulder" with plaque and drilling tools. Before it was finally mounted, we had spent about three hours standing on a narrow ledge, beating on the granite boulder with drills.

In the meantime, Edwin Yeager, realizing that other people would also go to the shelter cabin rather than the summit, had another plaque made. This one was to be mounted on a rock near the shelter cabin where one might stand while gazing at the Mount of the Holy Cross. With the help of Karl F. Zeller, forest ranger from Minturn, we completed the mounting of the second plaque in August, 1963. Hopefully, now the plaques would be seen by all who climbed Notch Mountain.

Conditions for viewing the cross formation are generally at their best during the end of June and first part of July each year, a full six weeks earlier in the season than when Jackson photographed it in the 1870s and '80s. If one were to view the cross in the middle of August these days, he would find very little left of the formation, indicating that much heavier snowfall must have been normal in the period prior to the turn of the century.

Mount of the Holy Cross is no longer as elusive as it was in the past. In recent years two new excellent viewpoints have opened up to the public. A fine view of the 14,005 foot mountain is obtained from the top of the Eagle's Nest Gondola at the Vail ski area, and the west portal of the Eisenhower Tunnel on Interstate 70 gives an excellent distant view as well. Other places where one can drive an automobile in order to gain a view of the cross are Fremont Pass on Colorado Highway 91, Shrine Pass, the dirt road from Vail Pass to Redcliff and the summit of Mount

Evans, the nation's highest automobile highway. There is only one way, however, for one to view the entire cross formation: by climbing to the summit of Notch Mountain. All of the other viewpoints mentioned offer a view of the top half of the cross, at best. Notch Mountain itself is in the way and blocks the view of the lower portion of the formation.

The summit of Notch Mountain may be reached by turning west from U.S. Highway 24 at a point three miles south of Minturn on the road marked "Tigiwon and Halfmoon Campgrounds." These campgrounds are located in the White River National Forest about three and four miles from Highway 24 respectively. Camp Tigiwon offers a large log picnic shelter complete with huge fireplace in which one may spend the night if the weather is bad (it would be advisable to check at the White River National Forest ranger station in Minturn as to its availability beforehand).

The road comes to an end at the Halfmoon Campground and trailheads are located here. Past experience has shown that a lot of mosquito trouble might be encountered at Halfmoon due to the close proximity to several beaver ponds. For this reason I have found the lower Tigiwon campground to be more comfortable.

From the end of the road at Halfmoon Camp, take the one and a half mile trail to the top of Halfmoon Pass. Those who wish to climb Mount of the Holy Cross will continue on this trail down to East Cross Creek and then on up the mountain itself. For the view which Jackson photographed, one must leave the trail at Halfmoon Pass and follow an unmarked and partially obliterated trail up the north ridge of Notch Mountain. Shortly before reaching the top you will see the bronze plaque on the northwest side of the "Jackson Boulder."

To reach the shelter cabin, follow the left-hand trail from Halfmoon Campground which is marked "Notch Mountain and Lake Constantine Trail." About three miles from Halfmoon Camp, the trail splits. The right-hand trail will take you to the Notch Mountain shelter cabin, the left continues on to Lake Constantine and Tuhare Lakes, favorites among fishermen.

The six-mile trail to the shelter cabin is somewhat longer than the route to the summit via Halfmoon Pass, but is a much easier hike. Horses can easily be ridden to the Notch Shelter and can usually be hired from the stables at Vail and transported to Halfmoon Campground for you if so desired.

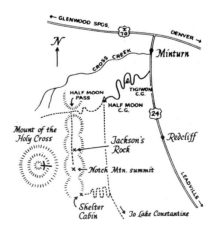

William H. Jackson Photograph - Colorado Historical Society Collection

CLOCKWISE FROM ABOVE: Clarence Jackson waving hat on "Jackson Boulder" as photographed by W.H. Jackson in 1893. Ken Barrow photographed on same boulder in 1958 by Ron Ruhoff. Ron attaching plaque.

Ron Ruhoff Photograph

Jack L. Morison Photograph

Over the years, much controversy has existed over the condition of the snowy cross formation. Since it is a known fact that William H. Jackson touched up many of his glass plate negatives to enhance the image and even went so far as to add an occasional item, such as a waterfall, that did not exist, many people wonder if the cross of snow ever was perfect in form. His famous 11x14 plate from August 23, 1873 has a non-existent waterfall showing below the cross and the cross itself shows signs of having been touched up. I decided to clarify this problem once and for all, so I went to the Colorado Historical Society archives and personally inspected many of the original Jackson glass plate negatives which are kept on file there. While some indeed did have touch-up work done on the arms of the cross, several others were not touched in any way, and even those showed the image of a perfect snowy cross.

Of the many photographs that have been taken of Mount of the Holy Cross through the years, none can compare with the perfect images which Jackson made with his bulky wet-plate camera in the 1870s. The mountain still offers one of the most breathtaking scenes in Colorado, and I highly recommend a trek to one of the two viewpoints on Notch Mountain in order to take in the full view of Colorado's Cross of Snow.

Ron Ruhoff Photograph

A Mount Evans

We're camped in the middle of a beautiful, untouched wilderness area. The scene is a high alpine lake, which, at this late afternoon hour, is a clear pool of liquid silver and gold reflecting a large cumulonimbus cloud on the eastern horizon. Overhead, wisps of thin clouds are moving quickly across a bright crescent moon, which will soon set beyond the mountain ridge. The smell of campfire smoke mixed with that of fresh, frying fish drifts through the chill July air.

Music from a small tape player has brought a full symphony orchestra along with us to add a touch of magic to the scene. The selection is appropriately called "Mysterious Mountain". The term "mysterious" seems fitting at the moment because time, as we know it in the everyday hectic world, has drifted away from us much like smoke from the fire. A colorful rainbow has been perched on the edge of the huge cloud in the east, not moving for the last forty-five minutes. The close friendship of backpacking companions completes the good feeling of peace.

Perhaps this setting is familiar to some; possibly, others have only dreamed of such an experience. But I believe most are quick to assume that such a place exists only at remote distances from home, requiring at least several hours of driving plus many miles of rugged hiking to attain. Not so, for the above described scene actually existed during a recent summer, only 12 miles, as the crow flies, from my Evergreen, Colorado home in the newly established Mount Evans Wilderness Area.

Our three day back-packing experience finally became a reality after a couple of years of thought and some final planning early in 1981. I had been traveling much of Colorado for years and had packed into remote areas all over the state, but I will admit to being guilty of neglecting my own "back yard."

Friends and neighbors Clyde Coble, Jim Karuzas, Sid Phillips and I finally completed our plans. We would have three days to walk a twenty-mile route from the summit of Mount Evans to the end of the Meridian Trail near Brook Forest, via Bear Track, Roosevelt and Mud Lakes. As it turned out, weather and time cooperated perfectly with our plans.

Sid's wife Pat was our driver that first morning. The well-known drive up the Mount Evans highway was accented by a particularly beautiful view of the distant continental divide, a familiar place to us since we had recently made a project of hiking 100 miles of its actual ridge.

As we approached our drop-off point, about half-way between Summit Lake and the top, we were greeted by a number of shaggy white mountain goats who were still molting their winter coats. These beautiful and agile animals are not native Colo-

Mount Evans with the town of Evergreen and Evergreen Lake in the foreground.

Wilderness Adventure

by Ron Ruhoff

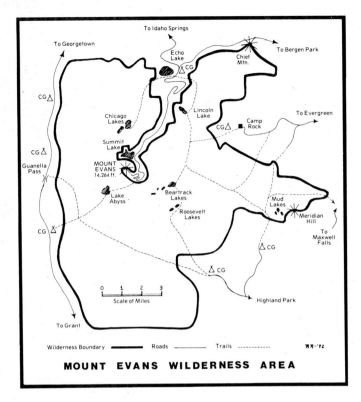

MOUNT EVANS WILDERNESS AREA

radans, but were introduced here from Montana a number of years ago. They are becoming increasingly familiar, along with the bighorn sheep, to those who drive the Mount Evans highway.

The car was parked at the place where you first look over the south shoulder of Mount Evans into South Park. Packs were donned in the chilly and windy morning air, goodbyes were exchanged, and we were on our way to a Mount Evans Wilderness Adventure. Of all the ways one can travel and camp out, nothing can compare to backpacking for a feeling of get-away-from-it-all freedom. There is something about having all your needs on your back that separates this sport from all others.

Jim could not find the time to join us for the beginning of the trip, but made plans to meet us at Mud Lakes the second afternoon. Clyde, Sid and I began the steep, rocky descent into the glacial cirques that contain the Beartrack and Little Beartrack Lakes. Since no actual trail exists here, one has to be cautious of the terrain, especially with overnight backpacks (ours averaged about 55 pounds).

The Beartracks are similar to hundreds of other alpine lakes that are set into the glacial cirques all along the eastern side of the Rockies. These blue-green jewels are remnants of the ice age when prevailing westerly winds would pile up snow of sufficient depth to form glaciers on the mountain ridges. The giant glaciers of those days actually gouged out the granite to leave impressive "east faces" on the mountains and natural dams of glacial moraine which contain the alpine lakes of today. A number of small, but significant, glaciers, such as St. Mary's, Arapaho, Isabelle and St. Vrain, remain in Colorado today.

The Beartrack Lakes consist of four small alpine ponds and the lower, or main lake, which is just below timberline. The largest of the lakes was our goal before heading over to the Roosevelt Lakes. When we reached the lake at about eleven in the

morning, our first thought was of fish. We unloaded the packs, getting out fishing gear, suntan lotion and food for lunch.

I can still remember Sid yelling, "Hey, wait a minute!" as he was unwinding his line. He had simply dropped his lure into the lake, preparing his rod for a first cast, when the fish struck. He caught it too, a nice, fat 10 inch native, or cutthroat, trout. This turned out to be only a prelude to some very fine fishing that day.

By 3 o'clock the three of us had enough fish for a fine dinner. It was tempting to stay longer, but we had a schedule to keep and wanted to allow enough time to get to the Roosevelts. We always hate to keep scheduls on vacation, but we did have a total of 20 miles of rough country to cover in order to get to the end of the trail where Clyde had parked his truck the day before, to provide for our transportation home. We also don't believe in being greedy about the fish—no use catching more than we could use, even though the limit would have allowed more.

We cleaned our catch, noting the salmon-like pink color of the meat due to their diet of freshwater shrimp which are found in these and many alpine lakes.

From the Beartracks we headed south along the established trail to Roosevelt Lakes. Just as we were rounding the hill near timberline, we saw a few cow elk ahead—this is their country and the Mount Evans elk herd is one of the largest in the state. We had noted the matted grass of several elk beds near the shores of the Beartracks that day.

The sun had long since set behind Mt. Rosalie as we approached the two beautiful little Roosevelt Lakes. Smoke indicated that the only other people we had seen all day since leaving the Mount Evans highway were camped here. By now, we knew, the usual bumper-to-bumper traffic would be heading down from the Mount Evans summit on its way back to Denver. We immediately set up camp, pitching our tents with flies in case of rain. A nearby storm was in progress and we could hear distant thunder. Our luck was with us, however, as the rain moved eastward and far enough south to leave us dry.

As we began our small campfire (wood is scarce here, as the Roosevelts are somewhat above timberline) in a metal grill someone had brought in, the magic of this Mount Evans Wilderness spot began to soak in. I had brought a small tape recorder, along with tapes of favorite music selections, and was now playing "Mysterious Mountain" by Alan Hovhaness.

The storm, which had recently passed us, was building up into tremendous thunderheads over the Denver plains, and had spawned a most beautiful rainbow which lasted, unchanged, for nearly an hour. All of this was reflected in the lower lake, creating, with our music, a place of timeless enchantment. I kept my camera busy while Clyde and Sid were frying fish. As the light on the big cloud faded to sunset orange, we opened a bottle of wine for the occasion and began to feast on fresh native trout. The tape continued, appropriately, with Schubert's "Trout Quintet."

The three of us ate all eleven fish and were just sitting back, in total darkness now, to enjoy the last drops of Mateus, when we heard footsteps in the distance and a voice calling, "Hey, Ron, that you there?" We were a bit startled at first—couldn't imagine who would be coming by that knew us. We soon realized that our friend, Jim, belonged to the voice. He found that he could get away sooner than originally thought and had his wife, Nan, drive him up to Mount Evans that evening. He then walked over Mt. Rosalie and on down to where he knew we were camped. Making plans and sticking to them can help at times, reminding us that hikers and backpackers should leave their "flight plans" with someone in case of unforeseen trouble.

We immediately felt bad about eating all the fish before Jim arrived, making it necessary for him to use his own pack food—instant oatmeal, I believe. He was definitely cheered up though, when Clyde mentioned the several pounds of frozen elk steaks he had brought along. That would make a fine breakfast the next morning.

We talked the rest of the evening, telling of our adventures that day and what was still in store for us on the trail ahead. We also got into a discussion about the newly established Mount Evans Wilderness Area, in the middle of which we were now camped, so very close to our Evergreen homes, and yet so remote and untouched.

We hoped that the status of "Wilderness" would not defeat itself by bringing in too many more people simply because of publicity about a wilderness area. This place always had been wild and relatively untouched—a new political designation did not make it so. The good side, though, might be limits on future overuse and misuse of the land, and emphasis on the need for increased education of all users to "do it right" by using minimum impact methods of camping and recreation.

Our meager supply of firewood finally ran out along with the thoughts, tall tales and wine, so we turned in for the night.

The morning dawned bright and clear with the promise of good hiking weather. I got out the camera first thing to capture a brilliant rising sun reflected in the lower Roosevelt Lake. Shooting directly into the sun like that can create interesting effects.

I was the only one to break out the fishing gear that morning for a round of the lakes, but the natives weren't hungry. Our hearts weren't really into fishing that day anyway, after eating so much the night before. Besides, the thought of elk steak and scrambled eggs for breakfast had our appetites worked up to a new high. The steak was fantastic— Chef Clyde had worked his magic on the little gas stove, and the four of us gorged ourselves anew with food from the land of Mount Evans. This time Jim didn't miss a thing!

Now it was time to clean up camp and stuff everything back into the backpacks. This, of course, included an empty wine bottle, pieces of trash foil and even a couple of old cans that someone had carelessly left behind at the lakes. This is part of the secret of maintaining a wilderness area—always adhere to the policy, "If you can pack it in, you can also pack it back out." If this little rule were followed by everyone, how much cleaner our land would be.

Our backs once again bore the load of pack gear as we left the lakes behind and headed up the trail toward the Pegmatite Points ridge. The name "pegmatite" refers to dykes or veins of granite. The ridge really didn't look as though it was far from camp, but it was a long, slow climb. Our recent studies in gastronomy must have had something to do with it.

Once atop the ridge, we were on the dividing line between the Pike and Arapaho National Forests. Approximately half of the Mount Evans Wilderness Area is managed by each forest under the U.S. Department of Agriculture. The views from here open up in all directions. We could see the Platte

Ron and Sid leave the Mount Evans Road on their way to the Bear Track Lakes.

19

ABOVE: Mountain goats on Mount Evans are members of a thriving herd originally introduced from Montana.

RIGHT: Roosevelt Lake and rainbow. The stark beauty of high altitude is often startling.

OPPOSITE: Morning light on Mount Evans is reflected in Mud Lake.

River Mountains to the south and could easily make out the location of South Park. The many homes of the Harris Park area could be seen in the distance below.

The trail we had followed since leaving Beartrack Lakes now headed south, down Tanglewood Creek to a confluence with Deer Creek at the Deer Creek Campground, an area accessible by road from Highway 285. From there we left the established path and headed eastward along the actual ridge to our next destination, Mud Lakes.

The summit of Rosedale Peak offered a fine panoramic view for our lunch stop that day. The term "lunch stop" isn't quite true in the usual sense of the word, because in hiking we tend to snack along the way with foods that offer high energy with a minimum of digestive work, rather than eating a heavy meal all at once.

Rosedale made a perfect viewpoint for exploration with binoculars and cameras. To the east we could see the Mud Lakes shining like silver mirrors beneath the rocky cliffs of Meridian Hill, our second-night campsight. It looked a long way off!

To the north we could see Longs Peak in Rocky Mountain National Park and to the west our starting point beneath the round, white dome of the Mount Evans observatory. Looking south, the entire Platte River Canyon country was laid out before us. From here on the ridge was not only the boundary between the national forests and the division between the Platte River and Bear Creek drainages, but the actual wilderness boundary as well.

The climb down from Rosedale to Meridian Hill Campground was steep, rocky and, in general, difficult with our large packs. The campground itself has nothing to offer in the way of man-made facilities except for an old aspen log lean-to which we promptly named "Le Chateau Meridienne". The campspot does have a delightful grove of aspen set in a natural pass over the ridge. The grove is a stopping point along the trail from Meridian Campground (near Highland Park), which crosses there on its way to Bear Creek. A cold spring of fresh water bubbles out of solid rock nearby, making this a very refreshing place to stop before completing the last mile to Mud Lakes.

Apparently, not many people hike over to Mud Lakes from Meridian Hill campground, because the trail was barely visible through the dense forest which contained a large quantity of windfall. We

Bear Track Lake on Mount Evans.

Ron Ruhoff Photograph

Ron, Sid and Clyde enjoy the view from Meridian Hill.

used old blaze marks on trees as a guide.

Suddenly, we broke out into the open and the Mud Lakes were before us. These Lakes are extremely shallow, probably no more than two or three feet deep, and are located in a large, beautiful meadow beneath Meridian Hill. We headed for the far side of the lakes and, among the trees, located a campsite with a fine view of Mount Evans. Storms were brewing above Evans by now and we thought it best to set up and be prepared for possible rain. Once tents were pitched we took our cooking pots to the lake for water to prepare dinners. We found that we had a ready-made soup of tiny shrimp which were so abundant in the water that we couldn't help bringing them back with us. There are no fish in these lakes, for they obviously freeze completely in winter.

We barely made it back to the tents before the rain began. It lasted through four solid hours of downpour, with nearby lightning and thunder. All of this is really "music of the mountains" and can be enjoyed as such if you are in a place safe from lightning and have a proper weatherproof tent. Each of us cooked personal meals that evening in our respective tents, making various soups, freeze-dried dinners and coffee with boiled lake water heated on the little pack stoves. We all slept like logs that night. It had been a long day with heavy packs.

The morning dawned crystal clear with heavy dew on the grassy meadow, and mist floating above the lakes, which offered a flawless reflection of Mount Evans. On the other side of the lake we saw several elk grazing peacefully. The wilderness enchantment was still working its magic.

Granola bars and scrambled eggs set off with shrimp-flavored coffee completed breakfast, and we soon were packed up and ready for the steep climb up Meridian Hill. Near the top we stood on some rock outcroppings which gave a perfect view of our entire route since leaving the Mount Evans highway two days before. We could easily make out the glacial cirques containing the Roosevelts and Beartracks, the lofty point of Rosedale Peak and the Mud Lakes straight below. The view seemed to sum up all of the wonderful feelings, views and adventures we had experienced thus far.

From Meridian Hill we still had about four and a half miles to go, a mile and a half of rock-hopping and dense forest, then easy going on the Meridian Trail. As we were skirting the cliffs on the North side of Meridian Hill, we came upon an old, lone mountain goat with one horn missing. He seemed to be on his own, probably rejected from the herd, but still standing majestically on "his mountain" as only an animal of his stature can.

We had barely reached the trail, which came up the ridge at this point from Bear Creek, when we met our good friend, Sid Whitford, coming toward us. He had known of our journey and hiked up just to join us and offer some refreshment in the form of a six-pack of some incredibly cold "Pure Rocky Mountain Spring Water." Now THERE'S a friend!

The last few miles went by quickly as we all talked about the events of the last three days. The truck was a welcome sight as the twenty-mile hike came to an end, but a poignant feeling of adventure had cast its spell on us all and plans were already taking shape for another trek into the Mount Evans Wilderness Area.

Pikes Peak Or Bust

by Jeremy Agnew

ikes Peak or Bust!'' That was the rallying cry of the 1859 gold rush to the Rocky Mountains of Colorado. Though the gold was actually found near present-day Denver, about 60 miles to the north, to the hopeful gold-seekers 14,110 foot high Pikes Peak became a symbol of hope for a new and better life, and of the fortunes to be found in the West.

Today, over a hundred years later, the snow-capped summit of Pikes Peak still looms majestically over Colorado Springs and the plains of eastern Colorado, and acts as a magnet for vacationers and sightseers from all over the country. Pikes Peak is not the highest peak in Colorado, but it is certainly one of the most impressive.

The peak was named for army Lieutenant Zebulon M. Pike, who discovered and unsuccessfully tried to climb the mountain in 1806, while leading a military expedition to explore the west following the Louisiana Purchase. After being thwarted by snow and bad weather, Pike emphatically stated that the mountain would never be climbed; however, it was conquered in 1820 by Dr. Edwin James, the botanist for a later exploratory expedition under Major

Stephen Long. Long left his name on Longs Peak in Rocky Mountain National Park.

Unlike the explorers of the early 1800s, the modern explorer, such as you or I, can ride effortlessly to the top of Pikes Peak in a streamlined, Swiss-built-diesel-electric railcar that ascends slopes so steep that it runs on a rack-and-pinion track.

If we prefer, we can ride 17 miles to the top in our automobile, in air-conditioned comfort, up the well-maintained Pikes Peak Highway. We would preferably drive at a leisurely pace on the way up, in order to enjoy the memorable views of the foothills and the plains far below. We would not want to follow the example of the professional race drivers who participate in the Pikes Peak Hill Climb on July 4th each year, sliding around the curves and switchbacks at speeds that reach over 100 miles per hour.

The really tough way to reach the top of the peak is to join in the Pikes Peak Marathon, a foot race enjoyed by those who have the stamina to run up 13 miles or so of Barr Trail to the summit and then turn around and run back down again. Among the various people who have journeyed to the top of Pikes Peak are a man pushing a wheelbarrow, a three year old

OPPOSITE: Pikes Peak rises above the red rocks of Garden of the Gods.

Jeremy Agnew Photograph

The lake at Crystal Park in the foothills above Manitou Springs.

Jeremy Agnew Photograph

Jeremy Agnew Photograph

Will Rogers Shrine of the Sun on Cheyenne Mountain.

OPPOSITE: The elegant and beautiful main hotel at the Broadmoor resort complex.

girl who walked each step of the way, a man who walked up on crutches, and an enterprising individual who, for reasons known only to himself, pushed a peanut all the way to the summit.

However you prefer to reach the summit, the trip is well worth it. On a clear day, it is possible to see the plains of Kansas to the east, the sagebrush of northern New Mexico to the south, and almost to Wyoming to the North. Behind you, to the west, the rugged backdrop of the Continental Divide pushes its snowcapped peaks into the clear blue Colorado sky. Appropriately, it was this view from the summit in 1893 that inspired Katherine Lee Bates to pen "America the Beautiful".

Apart from Pikes Peak itself, probably the best-known landmark of the Pikes Peak region is the Garden of the Gods in nearby Colorado Springs. Here in this 770 acre city-owned park, huge red and white rocks of sandstone stand on edge, a monument to the climactic birth of the Rocky Mountains. About 70 million years ago much of the North American continent was at the bottom of a vast inland sea. These sandstone slabs were deposited on the seabed, grain by grain, much as we find sandy ocean bottoms today. Then in one gigantic geological up-

heaval the sea bed was pushed up out of the way by the emerging granite core that today forms the Rocky Mountains. Wandering through the Garden of the Gods among these towering red slabs, the imaginative visitor can see camels kissing, a cathedral, a steamboat, and the face of the great Indian spirit Manitou etched into the contorted, wind-blasted rocks.

A little further west, similar soft easily-weathered rock formations have created the Cave of the Winds in Williams Canyon. Underground water, seeping through the limestone formations that make up the walls of the canyon, has created a series of tunnels and caverns that form a fantastic underground fairyland. Stalagmites and stalactites formed by dripping mineral waters are still growing towards each other drop by drop from ceiling to floor. Rock formations such as the Painted Curtain, the Bridal Chamber, and the Temple of Silence are comfortably visited on well lit paved walkways deep under the surface of the earth. Sparkling crystals of calcite and onyx are colorfully lighted to create fascinating displays.

Water was also the sculptor and still forms the scenic attraction at Seven Falls in South Cheyenne Canyon, to the southwest of Colorado Springs. This

canyon is billed as "the grandest mile of scenery in Colorado", and the drive up to the falls between the 1,000 foot high sheer granite walls that tower over the canyon and stream is indeed spectacular. The canyon ends at the falls themselves, which cascade 300 feet from pool to pool down a series of seven waterfalls. Those who have strong legs and plenty of breath can climb a steep flight of wooden steps that lead to the top of the falls and can enjoy the view back down into the canyon.

Near the top of the falls is the gravesite of author Helen Hunt Jackson, who wrote the popular 1884 novel *Ramona*, publicizing the plight of the American Indian. Her remains were later transferred to the Colorado Springs cemetery, but a plaque remains above the top of the falls to commemorate the site.

The best overall view of Seven Falls is from Eagle's Nest, an observation platform on the other side of the canyon, and reached by climbing yet another flight of stairs, or by riding in an inclined cable car.

Near Seven Falls is the Broadmoor, a huge resort that is more than just one of America's top-rated hotels. This sprawling complex was the conception of flamboyant Spencer Penrose, who prospered from gold mining in nearby Cripple Creek in the 1890s and then later went on to make his real fortune from copper mining in Utah.

In 1917, in a combination of shrewd business investment and philanthropy, Penrose bought and rebuilt a failing casino on the edge of Broadmoor Lake. Over the years the hotel complex has prospered and grown, and at various times, included a rodeo arena, a world-famous ice skating rink, three golf courses, a mountain lodge, a zoo, a riding academy, a ski area, an authentic English pub, and even a miniature narrow-gauge train that carried passengers on a two mile trip between the main part of the hotel and the zoo. Though some of these landmarks have come and gone with remodelling and rebuilding, the hotel complex still offers much for the vacationer.

As part of his expansion, Penrose built a zoo on nearby Cheyenne Mountain to house his private collection of animals. Over the years the Cheyenne Mountain Zoo has developed into one of the finest private zoos in the country. The buildings are attractively landscaped into the side of 9,225 foot Cheyenne Mountain, and scenic paths wind their ways through the outdoor enclosures. There are

OPPOSITE: Cadet Chapel at the United States Air Force Academy.

Jeremy Agnew Photograph

fascinating displays of gorillas, orangutans, penguins, lions, tigers, giraffes, bears, elephants and small mammals.

Just to the south of the zoo is Ski Broadmoor, a small but complete ski facility with chair lift, night skiing and a warming house with authentic German food. Further up the side of Cheyenne Mountain, above the zoo, is the Will Rogers Shrine of the Sun. Though Will Rogers is not buried there (he is buried in Oklahoma where he grew up), the 100 foot granite tower with its resonant chimes stands as a memorial to the beloved humorist.

To the north of the Broadmoor and five miles to the west of Colorado Springs, at the foot of Ute Pass, is Manitou Springs, in the center of many of the attractions of the Pikes Peak region. Surrounding the picturesque little town are such popular attractions as Van Briggle Pottery, the Cave of the Winds, the Mount Manitou Incline, the Pikes Peak Cog Railway, the North Pole and Santa's Workshop, the Hall of Presidents Wax Museum, the Garden of the Gods, and the Cliff Dwellings Museum.

Unlike Colorado Springs, which never actually had any springs, Manitou Springs was the site of more than fifty natural mineral springs. Ute, Cheyenne, Shoshone and Arapaho Indians came here to heal their battle wounds and cure their sick in these evil-smelling, bubbling mineral springs in the shadow of Pikes Peak. After the town of Manitou Springs was founded it became a fashionable spa and the springs attracted the ailing rich who bathed in the medicinal waters.

Up above Manitou Springs is Phantom Cliff Canyon, the site of the Manitou Cliff Dwellings Museum. Though there were never any cliff-dwelling Indians in the Pikes Peak region, this outdoor exhibit is an authentic reconstruction of the architectural styles of the early Indians of the southwest. In 1907 these ruins were carefully studied, dismantled, transported to Manitou Springs, then reassembled in this canyon from some privately-owned Indian ruins in southwestern Colorado.

To the west of Manitou Springs, the Mount Manitou Incline cable cars make a thrilling journey to the top of 9,455 foot Mount Manitou to give their riders a panoramic view of Manitou Springs and Colorado Springs. Near the top the grade of the tracks reaches 68%, which is enough to give even the most blase a thrill. The incline was built in 1907 to carry pipeline and construction materials for

waterlines and a hydro-electric plant on the south slope of Pikes Peak. When it had served this purpose it was opened as a tourist attraction.

In spite of all the natural attractions of the Pikes Peak region, the most popular tourist attraction in Colorado is completely man-made. Ten miles north of Colorado Springs is the 18,000 acre site of the United States Air Force Academy. The purpose of the academy is to train young men and women in leadership, and to teach them the professional skills needed as officers in the United States Air Force. The mountains towering up behind the buildings serve as a constant reminder of the strength and stature needed for our country's military leadership.

The focal point of the academy is the cadet area, which is itself dominated by the 150 foot tall cadet chapel, with 17 triangular glass and aluminum spires reaching up as if to pierce the sky. This imposing structure, completed in 1963, actually houses three separate chapels. The main body of the building is the 1200 seat Protestant chapel, while underneath is a 500 seat Roman Catholic chapel and a 100 seat Jewish chapel.

Following June Week and the graduation ceremonies, the cadet chapel is the scene of many weddings. Cadets are not allowed to marry before graduation and, for many, the rewards of four hard years of study and work are a second lieutenant's bars and a gold wedding ring.

The futuristic glass and metal designs of the Air Force Academy contrast sharply, but harmoniously, with the surrounding mountains and with the rolling hills of the grounds, covered with pine trees, that are home to the academy's resident herd of mule deer.

About ten miles north of the Air Force Academy is the town of Palmer Lake. When Major Steven Long's expedition was exploring the Pikes Peak area in 1820, it was here that Dr. Edwin James, the botanist who first climbed Pikes Peak, discovered a tall, stately, white and lavender flower swaying gently in the breeze. This was the first record of the finding of the Colorado Blue Columbine. The early residents of Colorado were so impressed with the beauty of the columbine that, in 1899, it was adopted as the state flower. The deep blue of the columbine reminds Coloradans of the deep blue Colorado sky, the creamy white of the cup-shaped flower represents Colorado's snowcapped mountain peaks, and the yellow in the center represents the state's wealth in gold. The columbine indeed represents Colorado, and living and vacationing in Pikes Peak country.

Dwayne Easterling Photograph

At 7:58 a.m. on June 1, 1984 locomotives Number 8 and Number 14 ease out onto the high bridge, ninety-six feet above Clear Creek. Both engines whistled in triumph, announcing the return of steam to the Georgetown Loop.

t's not easy to find a time machine in this day and age, a time machine that can whisk one back into the roots of western American history. It's always possible to enter a museum and immerse oneself into the past, but as soon as you walk out the door, the present rushes back into place. But what if the museum were composed of an entire mountain canyon? What if, besides the historical interest, the museum sported a rushing mountain stream, towering peaks, lush pine and aspen growth, wildlife, and finally a commodity that too many of us are missing in our lives: fresh, clean mountain air. Such a museum exists. The sights, sounds, smells and joys of Colorado's vibrant past and magnificent mountain vistas come together in the Georgetown-Silver Plume National Historical District.

The centerpiece of the entire district is the towering Devil's Gate Viaduct, the high bridge of the Georgetown Loop Railroad. The original bridge was torn down and sold for scrap in 1939.

You don't know what you have until it's gone. Many in Colorado did come to regret the closing of a chapter in the state's heritage. Fortunately, development never encroached into the valley. Only minor changes had occurred over the years. As early as the late fifties, the idea to restore the area came to some farsighted individuals. Finally, on June 1, 1984, at 7:58 A.M. the impossible happened. Steam engines number 8 and 14, two shay geared type locomotives, backed down from the Silver Plume station. They slowly, but confidently edged out onto the steel of the high bridge, ninety-six feet above rushing Clear Creek. First number 8 whistled, then number 14 answered and then both whistled in triumph. The sounds echoed off the canyon walls and back through time. Once again, the Loop lives!

A SHORT HISTORY

Hundreds of years before the white man first crossed the Mississippi River, gold was rumored to be in the "Shining Mountains" of what was to become Colorado. The Spanish explorer, Coronado, acting on stories the Indians told, looked for the "Seven Cities of Cibola", finding nothing but dry hostile plains, cold, wind-swept mountain peaks, and little else. They returned to Mexico City with only a few maps they had made along the way, and more stories about the gold they could not find.

With the Louisiana Purchase in 1803, the government of the United States sent expeditions into the area to find out just what they had purchased. One of them, led by Lieutenant Zebulon Pike in 1806, tried to climb the most prominent peak in the area, but failed. Not wanting to depart without leaving some imprint on the mountain, he named it after himself. Pike's Peak became the main landmark that future pilgrims looked for when they were headed toward the gold diggings of Colorado.

With the discovery of gold at Sutter's Mill, on the western slope of the Sierras, in 1848, the rush to the Rocky Mountains was stalled for ten years. Of the thousands of men who headed to the California gold fields only a few were to strike it rich. The Russell brothers, Green, Levi and Oliver were some of the disappointed gold seekers. They had returned to their native Georgia in 1852 after having little luck prospecting for gold in California. But when they received word of gold in the Rockies the lure was too much and they set off again.

They arrived in 1858 to once again try their luck. They panned the low lying streams at the foot of the Rockies, but found only small amounts of gold dust. Green Russell decided to head into the mountains to

The Georgetown Loop, Rebuilding The Past

by Jim Wild and Dwayne Easterling

Georgetown Breckenridge & Leadville

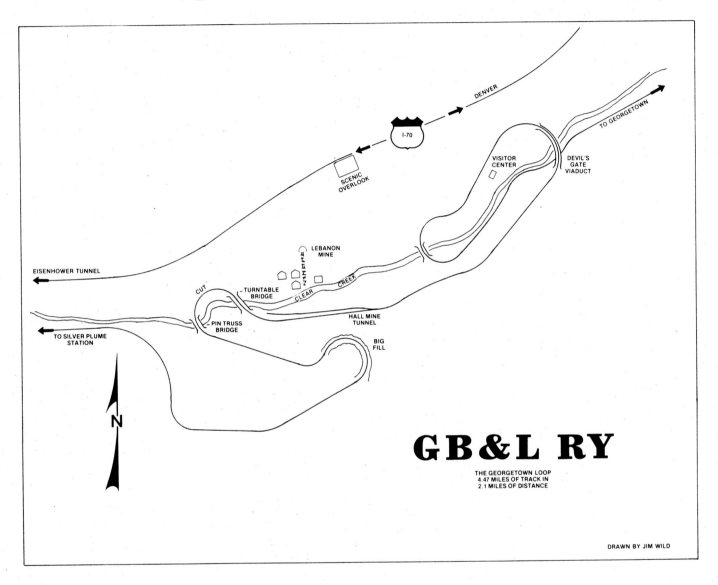

EISENHOWER TUNNEL

TO SILVER PLUME STATION

DENVER

I-70

SCENIC OVERLOOK

VISITOR CENTER

DEVIL'S GATE VIADUCT

TO GEORGETOWN

LEBANON MINE

CUT

TURNTABLE BRIDGE

CLEAR CREEK

PIN TRUSS BRIDGE

HALL MINE TUNNEL

BIG FILL

N

GB&L RY

THE GEORGETOWN LOOP
4.47 MILES OF TRACK IN
2.1 MILES OF DISTANCE

DRAWN BY JIM WILD

OPPOSITE: With the tumbling waters of Clear Creek below, consolidation, Number 40 backs slowly across the new Devil's Gate Viaduct.

Dwayne Easterling Photograph

Shay locomotives Number 8 and Number 14 simmer in the dawn light as the crew prepares for a new day of operation on the Georgetown Loop Railway.

find the large deposits that were locked in sandbars farther up the Platte River. He followed the river for about eight miles working the more promising sandbars. Finally Russell and his party found a sandbar that yielded about twenty dollars per day per man. This was why they had come to the Rockies. His hopes had been proven correct. The deeper they went into the mountains, the more gold they found.

Word of the Russell brothers' discovery travelled fast. Many others followed them into the foothills and by winter of 1859 a bustling mining camp was located on the banks of Cherry Creek.

One of those who arrived at this time was a gold fevered muleskinner named John H. Gregory. He and a group from Indiana followed the north fork of Clear Creek nearly to its head waters. On May 6, 1859 Gregory found decomposed quartz that appeared very similar to that of his native Georgia. The men began to dig in the "blossom rock". After a few feet his pick hit softer material. Gregory took a pan full of the rock to the river. As he washed away the dirt in the cold mountain water, grain after grain of pure gold was exposed in his pan. During the next five days he washed out of his vein $972, and the rush to Gregory Gulch and Clear Creek was on. In the following three years, Gregory and the thousands of other prospectors who followed took out over two and a half million dollars from the banks of Clear Creek.

Those who had arrived too late to stake their own

claims either left to look in other areas or went to work for the lucky ones who had already found gold. One of the late comers who decided to look elsewhere was George Griffith. Heading back down to the forks on Clear Creek he proceeded to follow the south branch of the stream to the mining camp which was to become Idaho Springs. Finding much the same story here that he had at the Gregory Gulch diggings, Griffith went further up the valley. At a wide area in the canyon he stopped to rest and contemplate his situation. As he was considering his position he looked up to see what appeared to be an interesting rock outcropping. Upon further examination he found what looked like gold ore. George went to get his brother, who was working in a mine in Central City. They began to work the outcropping and in a very short time had produced a little over five hundred dollars worth of gold ore.

The news of a gold discovery travels fast. In no time at all a new town had sprung up in the little valley and George's Town was born. Very little gold was found in the area, however, and there was concern that Georgetown would become the area's first ghost town. In 1864, a little west of the original Griffith discovery, James Huff made the first find of what was to become the area's main product, silver. In the years of 1860 through 1893 the Georgetown area produced more silver than any region in the world. Over $210,000,000 worth of silver, gold, lead, and other metals were produced by the Georgetown mines. Some say there is at least that much still left in the ground.

Transportation was one of the big problems for the mine owner. No matter how much gold and silver ore his mine was producing, if he could not get the ore to the smelter he would not realize a profit. The only way the Huffs and Griffiths of the day could ship their ore was on the backs of mules, and later, after roads were built, in large ore wagons. Some of the early towns built their own smelters but there was still the need to get the ore out of the mountains economically. Only the best producing mines could afford to ship through the teamsters and their ore wagons. Mines that did not produce the highest grade ore generally shut down simply because shipping costs were so high. The high cost of transportation affected everyone in the mountains. The store owner had to pass on the inflated costs to his customers. In the days of two dollar a day labor, every cost reducing means had to be considered.

As the mountain towns began to prosper other towns on the plains to the east did also. They were not mining towns but acted as supply centers for the mining towns in the mountains. Many times during the early days of the Colorado Territory some enterprising person would build a toll road into the mountains to serve the Central Cities and Georgetowns. Of course a fee was charged to use the road. This made shipping easier but did not do much to reduce shipping prices.

One such enterprising soul was William A.H.

Loveland. He had come to Colorado Territory in 1859 to open a dry goods store. Loveland settled in what was to become Golden, and had a hand in forming the town. His dry goods store did well and in short order he was one of the leading citizens of the fledgling town. But Loveland had grander plans than operating a mercantile business.

With all the traffic through Golden, Loveland soon realized that a railroad into the mountains and possibly clear to the west coast was needed. The Union Pacific and Central Pacific were building toward the first transcontinental meeting, and Loveland had plans for having them cross the mountains through Clear Creek and Golden. All he needed was a route.

With this in mind Loveland and some other Golden merchants incorporated the Apex & Gregory Wagon Road Company in 1861. The problem of having a wagon road company and no road was solved by contracting with Edward L. Berthoud, a young Swiss civil engineer, to plan a route into the mountains by which a toll road and later a railroad could be built. The first phase would be to build to Black Hawk and Central City. These towns were already bustling centers of activity and serving them would help Loveland's financial position. Of course the main idea was to ultimately build over the mountains, and on to the west coast.

Berthoud had been in the area for a few years and had been to the mountain towns. He had known Loveland since arriving in Golden, and wanted to see his town attract a transcontinental railroad. There was also one other reason for a railroad. Golden and Denver were the two main towns on the eastern side of the Rockies and a rivalry had developed between the two fledgling cities. Everyone knew that sooner or later Colorado would become a state but which of the two would be the state capital? Golden for a time had been the Territorial Capital but that honor had been taken by Denver. Golden wanted to get even.

Berthoud set out in 1861 with the old mountain man Jim Bridger to look for a pass through the Rockies. It didn't take them long to find one, and today it bears the name Berthoud Pass. Arriving back in Golden with Jim Bridger he reported to Loveland and his associates that they had found an old Indian trail which took them over the Continental Divide. Loveland now had a route, but could not start

Conductor, Lea Ashby, inspects the couplers of her train before departing Silver Plume.

Number 40 rounds the last curve on its way to Silver Plume for the last run of the day.

building. Because of financial problems it was to take more than a year before anything could be done.

Loveland incorporated the Clear Creek and Guy Gulch Wagon Road Company. The idea was the same, to build into the mining region, but this time it was really just a preliminary toward building a railroad. He felt that having an operating railroad already in the mountains would just about guarantee the support of the Union Pacific Railroad.

Loveland and lawyer Henry Teller went to the directors of the Union Pacific with their plan. They would be ready to push into the mountains whenever the first rails reached Golden. Loveland had secured a charter from the territorial legislature to build the Colorado Central and Pacific Railroad. With the two major rail lines building to span the nation it seemed unlikely that Loveland had any serious thoughts of building to the Pacific, but any self respecting rail baron of the day put "Pacific" in the corporate name to impress the investors.

The Union Pacific people listened attentively to the proposed plan and turned it down cold. They were not the least bit interested in building over thirteen thousand foot peaks when the vast flat lands of Wyoming were just a hundred miles to the north. They informed Loveland and Teller that they were in a race with the Central Pacific to build across the nation, and whoever built the most track received the most money. Since the Central Pacific had to build through the Sierra Nevada the UP officials felt that they had a distinct advantage and they weren't about to even the score, so to speak, by building through their own mountain range when they didn't have to.

This left Loveland and his associates, and all of Colorado for that matter, with its multimillion dollar mines high and dry as far as being on the transcontinental railroad.

Later the UP was to have a change of mind, of sorts, and helped bring a feeder line down to Denver from Cheyenne, but this didn't do a thing for Loveland and his plans to have Golden the economic hub of Colorado. They had lost out to Denver in terms of being on a direct hook up with the UP, but they would not lose out when it came to tapping the rich mining districts to the west.

In 1871, with a $250,000 bond issue from Central City and Black Hawk, Loveland's group began laying track into the mountains. In just seventeen months they reached the outskirts of Black Hawk, not a bad time frame considering the terrain they had to build through. The effects of the railroad were immediately felt by all those involved. Freight costs dropped about 60 percent, store owners no longer had to inflate prices because of high shipping costs, and the lower grade mines could once again be operated at a profit.

While the mine owners and merchants of Central City and Black Hawk were basking in the pleasures of having a rail connection with the outside world, their compatriots in Georgetown were not so well blessed. True, they didn't have to go as far as they once did to reach rail traffic, but they didn't have an immediate outlet for their goods.

The Financial Panic of 1873 was being felt in Colorado and just about all railroad construction had been stopped. By the time the money situation had improved enough to once again allow railroad construction, Loveland and his associates had to fight off creditors of the financially troubled little railroad. The Colorado Central survived these trying times but was still short on money to build any further. "Help" arrived in the form of Jay Gould and the Union Pacific. Gould made arrangements that would place the Colorado Central under UP control. He placed Loveland in control of the line and made funds available to complete the railroad into Georgetown. On August 13, 1877 the first train ran up to the new brick station, and Georgetown finally had its rail connection.

In 1879 the Colorado Central became an official part of the Union Pacific Railroad. They leased the Colorado Central for 50 years. Gould arrived in October to tour his new holdings. While touring the system he spoke of plans that were to bring tears of joy to Loveland. Gould wanted to build to Leadville.

JULY.

TOURIST'S

Thumb Nail

FOLDER

SHOWING THE

UNION PACIFIC

RAIL WAY.

RESORTS AND ROUTES IN COLORADO

GEO. ADY, Gen'l Agent Passenger Dep., - Denver Colo.
D. L. STURGIS, City Pass-nger Agent, - "
B. P. M. KIMBALL, City Tkt. Agt., 1703 Larimer St., "
E. F. LACKNER, Depot Ticket Agent, - - "

Before a railroad could be built to the fabulously wealthy and isolated Leadville there were a couple of problems to overcome. One was that there was an elevation difference of 638 feet and only 2.1 miles between Georgetown and Silver Plume. The other was that the steep mountain walls would not allow the use of switchbacks to gain elevation.

The Union Pacific brought in engineer Robert Blickensderfer. He devised a plan to lengthen the line to about four and a half miles and loop the track back over itself to cut the grade to three and a half percent. About two hundred men were engaged in grading and laying track on the Loop Line. But progress was slow due to the fact that the men wouldn't stay on the job. Many out of work men would sign on to work on the grading and track laying, but once they had received free transportation to the gold fields and gotten a meal and a little money they would take off to seek their fortunes. This situation would have a dire effect on the Union Pacific.

In order to finish the rail line to Silver Plume and beyond, the Union Pacific incorporated a new railroad, the Georgetown, Breckenridge & Leadville. This railroad was to start construction at end-of-track at Georgetown and take the line over or under, they weren't sure at this point, the Loveland Pass route. The Union Pacific had long since discarded Berthoud's survey as being totally impractical. His proposed line was just too steep and high.

The most impressive thing about the entire railroad was to be the high bridge or Devil's Gate Viaduct. A contract was awarded to the firm of Clark Reeves & Company of Phoenixville, Pa. for the erection of the bridge. Clark Reeves & Co. didn't have any better luck recruiting qualified help than did the railroad. When the bridge was completed, Robert B. Stanton, the railroad's chief engineer, refused to accept the bridge. He found poor workmanship and defective riveting to be the main problems. The railroad and the contractor entered into negotiations to reach a satisfactory solution to these problems. Since the railroad controlled the payment for the work done, Clark Reeves & Co. saw the wisdom of repairing the bridge to the satisfaction of the railroad. This was done in short order and this time the railroad accepted the bridge. By January 23, 1884 the repair work was completed. The "High Bridge" proved to be sturdy and substantial. It served the railroad for over fifty years with very little maintenance. The only attention the bridge received was the addition of some bracing to accommodate heavier locomotives in 1921.

The cost of the Georgetown extension was $254,700. This included the cost of the High Bridge. The bridge itself was 300 feet long and consisted of eight thirty foot long iron plate girder spans and one sixty foot iron lattice girder span. It was built on an 18 degree 30 minute curve and was on a two percent grade. The height was seventy-five feet above the lower track, and ninety-six feet above the tumbling waters of Clear Creek.

Denver, Idaho Springs, Silver Plume
THE GEORGETOWN LOOP LINE—Narrow Gauge

READ DOWN — Trains 51 and 54 effective June 1st. — READ UP

51 Daily	53 Daily	Miles	TABLE No. 5	Elevation	52 Daily Ex. Sun.	56 Sun. Only	54 Daily
AM	PM				AM	AM	PM
8 10	3.15	0.0	Lv..Denver (Union Station)..Ar	5183	10 20	11 25	6 15
f 8 19	f 3.24	2.1	"..........Argo..........Lv	5225	f10 10	f11 15	f 6 05
		2.6	"....Clear Creek Junction...."	5232			
8 36	3.41	7.6	"..........Arvada.........."	5330	9 52	10 57	4 47
f	f	9.4	"..........Ridge.........."	5420	f	f	f
f 8 45	f 3.50	11.2	"..........Mt. Olivet.........."	5495	f 9 41	f10 46	f 4 37
f	f	13.3	"..........Wiggington.........."	5585	f	f	f
8 57	4.02	15.9	"..........Golden.........."	5691	9 27	10 32	4 25
f 9 10	f 4.13	18.9	"....Chimney Gulch.........."	5920	f 9 15	f10 20	f 4 13
f 9 22	f 4.23	21.9	"..........Guy Gulch.........."	6221	f 9 05	f10 10	f 4 02
f	f	23.4	"..........Beaver Brook........"	6400	f	f	f
f 9 36	f 4.41	24.5	"..........Elk Creek........"	6533	f 8 56	f10 01	f 3 52
f 9 47	f 4.53	26.8	"..........Roscoe........"	6768	f 8 45	f 9 50	f 3 42
f 9 51		27.8	"..........Big Hill........"	6832	f 8 41	f 9 46	f 3 38
9 55	5.00	28.7	Ar }..Forks Creek..{ Lv	6888	8 38	9 43	3 35
10 05	5.10		"	6888	8 33	9 38	3 28
f10 17	f 5.22	32.1	"..........Floyd Hill.........."	7207	f 8 23	f 9 28	f 3 18
10 37	5.41	37.4	Ar }..Idaho Springs..{ Lv	7549	8 06	9 11	3 01
10 37	5.41		Lv	7549	8 06	9 11	3 01
f10 42	f 5.45	38.7	"..........Stanley Mines..........Lv	7634	f 7 59	9 04	f 2 54
		38.9	"..........Stanley Mill..........	7644			
f10 46	f 5.49	39.6	"..........Fall River..."	7682	f 7 56	f 9 01	f 2 51
f10 55	f 5.58	42.1	"....Dumont...."	7935	f 7 48	f 8 53	f 2 45
f11 02	f 6.06	44.2	"....Lawson...."	8118	f 7 42	f 8 47	f 2 37
11 06	6.11	45.7	"....Empire...."	8245	f 7 37	8 42	2 32
11 25	6.26	49.9	"..........Georgetown...."	8480	7 22	8 27	2 17
			(The Loop)				
11 50	6.50	54.0	Ar......Silver Plume.....Lv	9114	7 05	8 10	2 00
AM	PM				AM	AM	PM

DAVID S. DIGERNESS COLLECTION

Rail was eventually run to the little town of Graymount, about four miles west of Silver Plume. Here all rail activity stopped. The grand plan to push the railroad over or under Loveland Pass was never completed. The Union Pacific had acquired another railroad, the Denver, South Park & Pacific, and it had been run into Leadville over a much easier pass than Loveland. There was no need to have two railroads owned by the same people serving the Leadville Mining District.

In a state that is itself a "scenic wonder", to call one item by that name seems a little presumptive. But that is what the Union Pacific did. They realized that the Devil's Gate Viaduct was something people from all over the nation would want to see. Advertisements promoting "Colorado's Scenic Wonder" were taken out in all the newspapers of the day. The mining boom was beginning to level off by the time the railroad reached Silver Plume and the Union Pacific wanted to get its money's worth from the project.

In 1890 the Union Pacific merged its seven subsidiaries into one railroad, the Union Pacific, Denver & Gulf Railroad, in an attempt to operate in a more financially efficient manner, but money problems were to continue to plague the UP. Finally, after years of financial difficulties, the Union Pacific fell into receivership. Out of the failure came a new railroad in 1899, the Colorado & Southern.

The C&S took advantage of the Loop Line in its advertisements, promoting the thrill and excitement, and minimum cost, of riding the "Great Georgetown Loop". Many photographers of the day made quite a tidy sum selling post cards and photographs of the daring passengers as they travelled over the Loop. To test their bravery, men were persuaded to walk across the bridge, and women swooned as they gingerly made their way over.

Shay locomotive Number 8 and 2-8-0 locomotive
Number 40 meet at Hall Tunnel siding. The tunnel
was once a producing mine.

The Loop trip was certainly a success. At its peak, seven trains a day made the trip from Denver to Silver Plume. The C&S built a pavilion between the wye tracks at Silver Plume to accommodate the needs of the passengers. In the early days of its operation dinner was only seventy-five cents. There were other things for the intrepid rail passenger of the day to do. The Sunrise Peak Aerial Tramway took passengers to the top of Sunrise Peak in gondolas. The Argentine Central was a twisting rail line that left from Silver Plume and went to the top of Mt. McClellan. The proposed reason for the Argentine Central was to serve the mines on the mountain, but in actuality, hauling passengers to the top of the mountain brought in more money than the mining activities ever did. Both of these were gone by 1920.

For a number of years after the completion of the Loop Line the passenger fares literally held the railroad together. The Colorado & Southern operated two passenger trains a day from Denver. On Sunday during the summer season a "fisherman's special" was run up the canyon. This train would drop off anglers at various spots along the way and pick them up later in the afternoon. One wonders, with all the minerals running down Clear Creek from the mining activities in the area, just how successful the fishermen were. Another popular feature the railroad implemented was a dance pavilion at Beaver Brook. The C&S hauled a band and passengers to this location for an afternoon's entertainment.

All things must come to an end and so it was for the Colorado & Southern narrow gauge operations. The improvement of roads and the increasing use of the automobile were making themselves felt by the early 1900s. Passenger service slipped to only two trains a week by 1910 and just ten years later were almost discontinued altogether. What passenger service was needed was added to whatever freight train was headed up the canyon. By 1930 even the mixed train was a thing of the past. Any traveler wishing to go to Central City or Georgetown had to ride in the tiny caboose with the crew.

The mines of Clear Creek had all but stopped production, and those that remained had generally turned to trucks to haul their ore from the mountains. This left the railroad in a very precarious position. It was losing money at a record pace. The narrow gauge operations were a financial drain on the rest of the system, and this could not go on for long.

The railroad made application to the Public Utilities Commission to abandon the line, and a few months later they received approval. First to go was the line from Central City to Black Hawk. Then in 1939 the line from Silver Plume to Idaho Springs was pulled up. The High Bridge was sold to the Silver Plume Mine & Mill Company for $450.00, and was to be used for mine supports in the area.

Most of the narrow gauge locomotives were scrapped, but a few remain. The Number 71 was given to Central City, and the Number 60 was placed on display at Idaho Springs. Number 9 found its way to Hill City, South Dakota, where it can be seen today.

Cornelius W. Hauck in his book NARROW GAUGE TO CENTRAL AND SILVER PLUME (published by the Colorado Railroad Museum) best summed up the passing of the railroad:

"And so the little railroad - the first narrow gauge to push directly into the Rockies - was gone. It was mourned by some, but largely ignored in passing by most. It had contributed mightily to the area economy in its youth, and modestly in its old age; it had never been a burden to anyone except its conceivers and builders, Captain E.L. Berthoud, William A.H. Loveland and Henry Teller. It remains as a happy if fading memory with a place in the hearts of many."

THE PRESENT

The story of the present day Georgetown Loop Railroad actually had its beginnings in a neighboring mountain town. In 1968, a small group of businessmen decided to reconstruct part of the Colorado Central Railroad's trackage between Black Hawk and Central City. The first project was to find some steam engines for the line. One does not exactly go downtown to Crazy Ed's Used Car and Steam Engine Emporium to find this vanishing breed of machine. The hunt took on international aspects. Finally Lindsey Ashby, one of the principals, noticed in a newsletter from the Colorado Railroad Museum that there might be some engines available in El Salvador. He made the trip down and found, much to his delight, four engines from a narrow gauge Hawaiian railroad. Inquiries revealed that they were for sale for the very reasonable price of $2,500 each. He placed an order for three of them. After returning to Central City, a banquet was held to announce the acquisition of the engines. The very next morning, a letter arrived from South America with some bad news. It seems that the engines had suddenly gone

Dwayne Easterling Photograph

Ex-International Railway of Central America locomotive Number 40 passes over the 60 foot long iron lattice work span on the high bridge.

Dwayne Easterling Photograph

Shay locomotive Number 8 crosses the turntable bridge, the second of four bridges on the loop line.

up in value to $10,000 each. They had to write back with a polite "no thanks".

Then came word of several more engines on the International Railway of Central America that were available. The cost was $5,500 each. The engines were built in America by the famous Baldwin Shops. They were 2-8-0 Consolidation type engines. 2-8-0 means that there are two wheels under the pilot or cow catcher, eight driving wheels and no wheels under the cab. The engines are somewhat similar in appearance to much of the power that plied the rails of Colorado during the zenith of the narrow gauge era. Finally, the railroad had an engine. Although not verified, the owners heard that Number 44 steamed under her own power to the Mexican border. She was loaded onto a flatcar and made the trip to Rollinsville, Colorado on standard gauge trackage. The cost for moving the engine equaled the cost of the engine itself.

The group put a deposit on the other engine but several years passed without communication. The group decided that the engine was probably lost due to the changing political situation. However, in 1972, the phone rang. It was an acquaintance of the Ashby's who was searching for power for another tourist line. He called to say that there was a very nice engine with a tag on it reading "property of the Central City Railroad". Did they still want it? The answer was an emphatic "Yes!" One of the partners travelled down to accompany the engine on its journey to Colorado. A small diesel was used to pull Number 40 and several other pieces of equipment, but part way through the trip the diesel threw a circuit breaker and ground to a halt. Normally this presents no problem, but it soon became apparent that the crew assigned to the job had very little knowledge of the diesel that they were operating, so Number 40 was fired up and pulled the entire train, including the diesel, to the border. The biggest problem was finding water for the engine. Many stops at local wells were needed. The crew formed a bucket brigade to fill the tender. The owners have a photo of a very tired and dirty American businessman, in a suit, pouring a bucket of water into the tender.

The group, which consisted of Lindsey and Rosa Ashby, Don Grace, Dick Huckeby, and Dave Ropchan had previously discussed the possibility of becoming involved in the Colorado Historical Society's project in Georgetown. In 1973, they approached the state with their plan. They were awarded a 30 year contract to operate the Georgetown Loop Railroad.

That same year, one of those minor little miracles that make life worthwhile happened. It seems that the U.S. Navy's Reserve Mobile Construction Battalion, the "seabees", had come to the realization that none of the current units had any practical training in the art of building a railroad. Since the knowledge would prove invaluable during wartime, they were looking for work. They contacted the Historical Society and volunteered their services for building track and bridges. It was gratefully accepted.

Spring of 1973 saw the first two week summer camp for the Seabees in the area. They started grading the line, laying the first track in the Silver Plume yard and began work on the first of four bridges on the Loop. The bridge, a pin truss type, had been found on an abandoned Colorado and Southern branch. Photos of the old Loop showed that this bridge was nearly identical with the one originally used on the line.

At about the same time, the Historical Society discovered the second bridge near Denver. Originally built as a support for a turntable, the builders found that it was just the right length to span the river at the second crossing. This is the very bridge that was used originally. It was placed onto the original granite abutments that still remained in 1975.

The Union Pacific Railroad had been supporting the project from its inception. They donated two and a half miles of 70 pound rail. The Seabees began to lay the rail from the first bridge toward the Silver Plume yard. Engine Number 44 made the trip from Central City in 1974. During that same summer, the Seabees reached the yard. A ceremonial spike was driven to commemorate the event. Number 44 was fired up on a weekend in August that year, marking the return of steam to the valley.

Beside laying the track and building the bridges, the Seabees contributed in other ways. In 1975 the C&S depot in Silver Plume was moved to its present location. They then built the platform around the building. Of major importance was the rebuilding of the Lebanon mine structures near the turntable bridge. Faithful re-creations of the mine's outbuildings that were essential to the operation of the facility now await visitors. Lindsey Ashby recalls many weekends when the Seabees weren't in camp. He would arrive and find many of the men in their civilian clothes working to complete a project. Many of the fellows had become so involved that they spent considerable amounts of their own time working to complete the tasks. Commander Bob Feriter and the men of the Reserve Battalion #15 deserve a lot of credit for creating the valley museum.

Meanwhile, the railroad's owners still had the rail line in Central City to think about. Expansion toward Black Hawk had been halted. If the line followed the original trackage, a huge trestle spanning a gulch near the Mountain City site would have to be rebuilt. The expense would have been considerable. The decision was made to lay the track around the head of the gulch, circumventing the need for the bridge. A new problem arose with this decision. The radius for the curve would be very tight, even by narrow gauge standards. The Number 40 and the Number 44 are the conventional type of locomotive that one thinks of when visualizing steam engines. They have rods that attach each of the driving wheels to the

steam cylinders. This allows power to be transmitted to each set of wheels. The rod engines are the fastest of their genre, but the rods make the engines a bit stiff when negotiating tight curves. Another type of engine, known as a Shay, transfers power to the wheels through a series of pinion gears and universal joints. The engines are not nearly as fast, but can negotiate much smaller radius curves. While no shay engines regularly travelled the rails of the Colorado and Southern track in either Central City or Georgetown, they worked the rails nearby. The famous Gilpin Tram above Central City and the Argentine Central which met the tracks in Silver Plume both used the odd looking engines.

One of the last narrow gauge lines in existence to use shays was the Westside Lumber Co. in California. They had some of the largest and most powerful shays built. Lindsey Ashby located the ex-Westside shay Number 14 on the Camino, Cable and Northern, a small tourist railroad in California. The CC&N was about to lose its lease and cease operation. In 1975, Ashby was able to purchase the engine, several coaches, and a narrow gauge diesel. The 1943 era diesel originally came from Hawaii's Oahu Railway.

The original plan was to have the rod engines in Georgetown and the shay working in Central City, but the owners soon began to rethink their position regarding Central City. Expansion had become almost an impossibility. Right of way disputes with landowners toward Black Hawk loomed. The line could not progress any farther in the other direction either. The yards and the beautiful stone depot now lay buried under tons of mine tailings. The tailings pile with the two tiered parking lot can be seen just to the South of downtown Central City. The railroad was perched on the side of a hill above the town. There was just physically no room to do anything. Another problem lies with the mining history of the region. The area is literally honeycombed with old mine shafts and tunnels. Vibrations from the engine would travel along the labyrinth and shake foundations in the old town. The decision was made to concentrate on the Georgetown Loop. All remaining equipment was trucked to Silver Plume in 1981.

The owners knew that they should have another shay to go with the Number 14, so, before the switch to Georgetown, a search commenced. Another Westside shay, Number 8, had been purchased by a private collector. After extended negotiations, the collector reluctantly agreed to sell the engine. The deal stated that the Loop owners had one year to move the engine from Oregon to Colorado. The Number 8 was one of the largest three truck narrow gauge shays ever built. Trucking executives would look at her height and weight (154,400 lbs.), blanch white and refuse to even discuss the job. "Why that thing would flatten anything we have!" was the most oft heard comment. Finally, one year to the date after the agreement had been signed, Ashby and a friend arrived in Oregon with a specially outfitted trailer. Then began an odyssey across the country

Georgetown Loop Number 40 charges upgrade past the spur switch on its way to Silver Plume.

Dwayne Easterling Photograph

dealing with low overpasses, incredulous highway officials and a myriad of other problems that would fill another complete chapter. The shay finally arrived in Silver Plume during the 1978 season. The authors, while interviewing Mr. Ashby early in 1985, asked if he was satisfied with the four engines. "No, not at all. We're always keeping our ears open for any possibility." He paused a bit and smiled, "It's time for a new adventure!"

For several years, the trackage ended just short of the southern abutment for the high bridge. Cost on replacing the impressive structure was estimated at one million dollars. Then, another of those miracles happened. In 1982 The Colorado Historical Society announced that the Denver based Boettcher Foundation had agreed to a $1,000,000 grant. This was followed by grants of $400,000 from the Gates Foundation and $200,000 from the Atlantic Richfield Foundation. The combined monies have been used to build the Devil's Gate Viaduct, put in the fourth bridge over the river, and build the Society's visitor center at the base of the high bridge.

In 1984, 45,000 people rode behind the steam engines between Memorial Day and Labor Day. Many also took the guided tour of the Lebanon Mine and walked 600 feet into Republican Mountain. They stepped into the mine buildings and discovered tidbits of our heritage. They rode in the open gondola cars and got a view of the Rockies that is impossible from a steel and glass enclosed auto. Their hearts may have skipped a beat as the train eased onto the high bridge, experiencing the same thrill that passengers at the turn of the century felt. They may have talked with some of the railroad's employees and felt their love for what they were doing. They may have noticed on return trips that the employee roster stays the same. There is almost no turnover on the line. The "family" of people working on the railroad are very loyal. They may have gotten off the train and taken a walking tour of Georgetown. Some of the finest examples of the West's victorian architecture are found here. One fellow observed that the buildings in the town are so unique that half of them have been recreated as kits for model railroaders. The visitor may have extended his stay in the past with tours through the Hotel de Paris or the Hamill House Museums. They may have enjoyed a meal at one of the fine old eating establishments. If they were pressed for time, they may have simply slid back onto highway I-70 and continued on their way. That is the unique thing about the area. One can spend just an hour, or a full day, exploring and experiencing. One railroad man told Ashby, "You have it all here. This six mile round trip has encapsulated the essence of narrow gauge railroading and the history of Colorado."

Many groups and individuals have put in a lot of time and money to make the Georgetown Loop Historic District what it is today. The operating steam engines, forty-six pieces of narrow gauge rolling stock, and over three miles of track give today's traveller an excellent feel for what it was like to ride "Colorado's Scenic Wonder", The Georgetown Loop.

Dell A. McCoy Photograph

**Shay locomotive Number 8 is momentarily bathed
in sunlight before making the final curve into Silver
Plume, in this 1979 photograph.**

Ouzel Falls in Wild Basin.

The large man with the large cigar nearly filled the door as he walked into the art gallery. He strode purposefully up to the counter, shifted the cigar slightly and spoke.

"Well, we just drove through the national park to get here. What else is there to do in Estes Park?"

The man behind the counter just sighed and paused a bit before answering. His thoughts turned back several hours to the events of the morning. The sound of the alarm reverberating through the house had seemed almost sacrilegious at that hour. The sun was still an hour away from making an appearance. "But, such is the life of a wildlife photographer!" he had thought while groping for socks. Soon his small car was threading through the quiet streets of the village on the border of the National Park. The headlights picked out the forms of several mule deer that had ventured into the city limits. But deer weren't to be the photographic quarry today. He drove past the entrance station for the park, unmanned at this hour, and slowed. Peering into the darkness on either side of the road, his eyes searched for certain tell-tale shapes. The car climbed a short hill, rounded a curve and suddenly the expanse of Horseshoe Park lay ahead. Slowing to a crawl, his eyes strained into the black shadows, only occasionally flitting toward the deserted highway. Finally, on the opposite side of the meadow, he made out the shapes of what seemed to be elk. But, there was still no sign of the animal that he wanted in the viewfinder. The car slid quietly to a stop in a pulloff area near Sheep Lake. He sat and watched the dark forms of the elk slowly working their way toward the west. There seemed to be around fifteen of them, only a fraction of the three thousand residing within the National Park.

Besides being home for the elk, Horseshoe Park is also a prime area to spot bighorn sheep. The bighorn's natural habitat is high on the rocky slope to the north of the meadow. But the sheep require a great deal of salt in their diet. The soil below Sheep Lake is permeated with enough salt-like substances to attract the sheep. They will actually eat the soil to get at the salt. He knew that for several days the ewes and lambs had been seen in the meadow. Quite often, the rams will bed down on the slopes above

and watch the rest of the herd brave the valley. Eventually they come on down and have a mouthful of salty earth. That was what he was hoping for, a chance to photograph the rams. The photographer quietly slipped out of the car and sat on the hood to await the dawn. The air seemed to reach every depth of his lungs. Even in July, it held a hint of the winter which is always waiting in the wings at this altitude. The predawn gray of the sky was beginning to fade when he noticed a movement at Sheep Lake. A small group of deer had made their way to the shore to drink. The soft light now revealed that there were twenty elk in the herd across the way. Three of them were young bulls trying to be careful with their velvet antlers and yet look macho at the same time. A rock dislodged and clattered down the slope behind him. Turning, his breath caught as he saw the entire troop of bighorn making their way down. Suddenly a cottontail rabbit scurried for cover as a Great Horned Owl hooted in the distance. A myriad of birdsongs filled the air as the tips of the peaks to the west burst into the alpenglow of dawn. The photographer's head swiveled back and forth, trying to take it all in. His heart pounded with the excitement of a natural high. Just for an instant, he felt he was a part of the life within the meadow and not just a spectator. The spell broke, and he hurried for the camera. "This is just like 'Wild Kingdom' on television!" he thought. "The only thing missing is Marlon Perkins trying to sell me insurance!"

The national park system is like a series of 'Safety Islands' in our world. Progress, everyday worries and stress permeate the very air most of us breathe. But, the borders of the national parks valiantly strive to hold time back. Within those borders, the natural world is allowed to go about its own business with as little interference from man as possible. The effects are two-fold. First, scientists can study and learn in such a place. The second is that modern man has a refuge in which to replenish his sanity.

Rocky Mountain National Park in Northern Colorado is just such a place. The Utes and the Arapahos knew the area far before the white man invaded it. Bits and pieces of their passing can still be found. Evidence indicates that there were no permanent settlements in the Park. Rather, hunting parties ventured into the area. Traces of a major trail

Rocky Mountain National Park

by Dwayne Easterling   47

"Despite the ruggedness, these are friendly mountains. Short hikes can take you to alpine meadows and lakes that have delighted people for generations, yet remain protected and unchanged."
James Thompson, Park Supt.

CLOCKWISE FROM RIGHT: A lightning struck tree and a view of Longs Peak guard the beginning of the trail to Fern Lake. Colors both vibrant and subtle paint this scene of aspen and the forest floor. A diminutive blue sulphur butterfly alights on an alpine flower. Early morning sunlight touches a stand of aspen as the quiet waters of Hidden Valley Creek slip by.

Dwayne Easterling Photograph

Dwayne Easterling Photograph

48

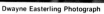
Dwayne Easterling Photograph

Dwayne Easterling Photograph

can be seen and hiked atop the tundra above timberline.

Trappers and settlers began to filter into the region around the 1860s. There was even a 'Jeremiah Johnson' type of resident mountain man known as Rocky Mountain Jim. Jim, it is said had only one good eye, the other side of his face had been left a mess after a disagreement with a bear. Women were said to faint at the sight of him.

One of the early characters that made a mark arrived in 1872 with a party of English sportsmen. Windham Thomas Wyndham-Quin, the Fourth Earl of Dunraven saw the beautiful land and decided that he wanted it. The wealthy Earl hired squatters to come in, claim a 160 acre tract and then 'sell' it to the Earl's company. He soon owned or controlled nearly 15,000 acres. Speculation was rampant that he wanted the area for his own private hunting reserve. The few landowners in the park bitterly resented the Earl. Among these was Rocky Mountain Jim, who held a tract that contained the main entrance to the Estes Valley. Eventually Jim was shot by the Earl's agent Griff Evans, but the steady influx of people into the area eventually defeated the Earl's plans.

Prospectors wandered through the mountains searching for gold, but the Front Range differs geologically from much of the Rockies. There just wasn't enough gold present to justify the expense of digging it out. So, the area never experienced a boom like Central City, Cripple Creek or Leadville. A few reminders still exist however. A small mine can be seen by hikers near the foot of the Longs Peak Trail. On the western side of the continental divide the last traces of Lulu City, a mining camp that struggled to survive a mere three years, awaits hikers.

People soon came to realize that the gold in this stretch of the Rockies was not to be found in the ground, but in the pockets of tourists. The noted naturalist and author Enos Mills led a long campaign to prevent total commercialization of the area. The fight was culminated on September 4, 1915 when the newest national park was dedicated.

One of Estes Park's most noted citizens during that period was F.O. Stanley, the inventor of the famed Stanley Steamer Automobile. Eleven passenger steamers would meet the train at Loveland, Lyons or Ward. Vacationers would then bounce over some rather terrible roads. Stanley's beautiful hotel and the wonders and grandeur of the national park soon made the traveler forget the harrowing drive.

The same grand view (and vastly improved roads), still await today's wanderers. 417 square miles of wilderness are traversed by three roads and over 355 miles of trails. Trail Ridge Road has gained justifiable fame as the highest continuous paved road in the country. It winds through three 'life zones' on its journey through the Park. The first is the Montane Forest, home of the mule deer population, lush meadows and stands of ponderosa pine. The next is the Subalpine Forest which marks the transition to a unique world. That world is the Alpine Tundra, the world above timberline. The road reaches its zenith at 12,183 feet above sea level, winding along the ridges that supply the name. The road was engineered to give a visitor a comprehensive view of the park and also facilitate spring snow removal.

Trail Ridge's predecessor still provides a thrill. Fall River Road, a one way dirt path that switchbacks much of its length, provides unforgettable views of the Park. Starting near the west end of Horseshoe Park, it eventually reaches the Alpine Visitor Center and rejoins Trail Ridge. A popular stop along the way is Chasm Falls.

The other road begins soon after the Beaver Meadows Entrance. It crosses the eastern edge of Moraine Park, then follows Glacier Creek. A large parking lot at the end of the highway provides access to one of the Park's jewels, Bear Lake.

The roads provide the complete Park experience for the majority of the visitors. The rangers are fond of stating that ninety percent of the Park's travelers see only ten percent of the area, and vice versa. For the other portion of the public, the roads are simply gateways to adventure. Here are some of the more popular trails:

PHANTOM VALLEY TRAILHEAD is located on the western side of the Park. The Colorado River is born within the confines of these mountains. Here, it is merely a small stream, nothing like the mighty river that inspires dams and power boats farther south. The trail follows the river on a flat and gentle floodplain. Along the way, one encounters a dazzling concentration of wildflowers. At about 1.4 miles, the tailings from a small mine appear on the slope above the trail. A scramble up the rocks will bring you to the entrance of Shipler Mine. This mine is safe to explore since it was carved from solid rock and has no hundred year old timbers supporting the mountain above. Standing in the entrance, with the breeze probing the tunnel, you can almost hear the straining muscles and quiet sighs of desperation from the solitary miner. Another .4 mile brings you to the remains of his cabins. At 3.1 miles from the trailhead, the broadening valley contains the site of Lulu City. Nature has almost completely reclaimed the area. Only faint traces of log foundations are now visible. But the same breeze that was at the mine sings sounds of the past to those who listen with their imagination.

WILD BASIN TRAILHEAD is located in the southeastern portion of the Park. It is not on one of the main Park roads, but is reached from State Hwy. 7. Therefore it is not as well traveled as many of the major park areas. After rounding Copeland Lake, a narrow road travels for two miles to the trailhead. A .3 mile walk through cathedral-like trees brings you to Copeland Falls. Actually, whoever named it was being rather optimistic since the 'Falls' could be mistaken for a large rapid. After another mile, the trail crosses North St. Vrain Creek on a large log bridge. The trail then starts up a slope toward

Calypso Cascades. Along the way, watch towards the south of the trail and you may spot a real oddity. An actual balanced rock left over from glacial times can be seen. The huge slab could support a bevy of square dancers on it. Most ''balanced'' rocks are products of erosion, but this is the real thing. Calypso Cascades is really a waterfall that is lying down. The steep mountainside is covered with a myriad of rivulets and rapids rushing towards a more gentle bed. This is one of nature's sights that is almost impossible to photograph. The feeling of the area cannot be compressed onto a 24x35mm piece of two dimensional film. But, it can of course, be placed on the great emulsion sheet of memory. At 2.7 miles from the trailhead, one of the most spectacular waterfalls in the Park churns over a cliff. Ouzel Falls, named for the small water bird seen flitting about the stream, can be a never forgotten target for a hiker.

BIERSTADT LAKE TRAILHEAD is located on the Bear Lake Road about six and a half miles from the entrance station. The trail switchbacks up a moraine that is covered with quaking aspen trees. This trail is a must during the autumn season when the trees have turned yellow-gold. The lake is 1.4 miles from the road and lies atop the hill just traversed. Fine reflections of Longs Peak and the Front Range tempt the lensman.

GLACIER GORGE TRAILHEAD is located on the Bear Lake Road less than a mile from the terminus. An easy hike of .6 miles takes one past beaver ponds, stands of aspen, a white water stream in a deep gorge and finally to Alberta Falls. The trail continues upward for 2.1 miles to The Loch. The author considers this to be one of the most beautiful lakes in the region.

THE BEAR LAKE TRAILHEADS. Many trails branch out from the popular Bear Lake area. For people with little time, there is a short nature trail around the lake. To the south, the trail to Nymph, Dream and Emerald Lakes is so well used, the Park Service has been forced to blacktop part of the path. Hikers that set their clocks early can usually avoid the rush however. Each lake is very scenic and is a worthy destination. The trail is also very popular with cross country skiers during the snow months.

The author's favorite trail starts on the north side of the lake. There seems to be a major attraction just around every corner for the length of the route. Two cars are beneficial here. Leave one at the Fern Lake Trailhead in Moraine Park, and take the other to Bear Lake. The trail climbs steadily away from the lake and skirts Flattop Mountain. Natural bouquets dot the landscape as you climb through the Sub-alpine Forest. Several lakes are seen before arriving at Lake Helene. Here, the trail takes a sharp turn down into Fern Canyon, crossing a talus slope alive with pika and marmots. Before descending, quickly scramble up the rocks to the right of the trail for a view that will be with you forever. Grace Falls tumble down the opposite slope. The eye wanders down the canyon past Odessa Lake and Fern Lake,

the goals of our hike. Fern Canyon is situated so that if there is a rain cloud in the area, the canyon will get wet. The result is similar to a rainforest in the Pacific Northwest. Plantlife is lush and colorful, and life abounds. Views of Little Matterhorn and Notchtop Mountain will activate your shutter finger. It is easy to spot Brook Trout gliding in the waters of Fern Lake. After a lunch stop at the lake, the hiker continues down the sloping trail to Fern Falls. The next stop is The Pool on the Big Thompson River. The trail flattens out and follows the river and its many beaver ponds. One last attraction is the unique Arch Rocks which look like they could have come from the moon (or at least Arizona). The trail is 8.5 miles in length, but after the first climb out of Bear Lake, it is mostly downhill.

These are but a few of the treasures to be found in Rocky Mountain National Park. Yet the question remains. Just what is there to do here? The answer lies waiting in many places. It may be found in the delicate pastels of a wildflower pushing impatiently out of a snowbank. It may come late at night, carried on the wind with a coyote's howl. The sound is at once romantic and yet carries a touch of Hitchcock that vibrates some primordial nerve. It may be found in the Time that is etched into the geology of the rock. A hundred years to a granite cliff is like a minute to mankind. It may be in the wonder at discovering the very life in the tiniest twig. It may be in the thrill singing in the backbone when you hear your first elk bugle. It may be in the serenity, yet strength, of a bighorn ram's gaze. Or, it may be in the discovery of self, as expressed in these words originally penned onto sweat soaked paper atop a mountain:

''There are two distinct types of 'being tired'. The first type is the fatigue brought on by a long day at the factory, or the kitchen, or the office... This is the malady so common to many Americans. The ache of toiling at an unloved job. You are there because bills have to be paid, kids have to be raised, responsibilities have to be met. 'Man, I hate this job!' The tiredness that this creates can prove to be fatal, for it is mostly mental.

''The other type of 'tired' is like a religious experience. It's what you feel after finally reaching the top of a 12,000 foot mountain. Every muscle cell and nerve ending harbors tiny pains. Your feet feel like one solid blister. A range of mosquito bites traverse your neck and arms. Dried sweat chafes under the heavy pack. 'But, by God! I made it! Me! Myself! With no motor except my brain to propel me. No wheels except my legs to get me here! Slush on, O potbellied mankind! I've made it!' This is the 'tired' that breeds contentment.''

So what is there to do here? If you have to ask, you probably wouldn't understand the answer. What happened to the large man with the large cigar? I simply handed him a map with the nearest route to Las Vegas. He left shaking his head. I'm sure we both were feeling a little sorry for the other, knowing that we could never understand that kind of thinking.

ABOVE: A young red tail hawk exercises his wings.

The pika, a small relative of the rabbit, lives in rocks near timberline.

ABOVE: A group of bighorn at Sheep Lake in Horseshoe Park.

RIGHT: A magnificent bull elk surveys his realm.

BELOW: A mule deer buck grazes near the Fall River entrance station.

53

Rumors that gold had been found in the western part of Kansas Territory had circulated among the eastern states for more than two decades prior to 1859. Zebulon Pike's journals had mentioned it, and various mountain men on their annual treks to St. Louis claimed to have observed golden particles in the beds of western rivers. President Lincoln's friend, William Gilpin, said that he had seen gold while traveling with John C. Fremont. Although the rumors persisted as a subject of eastern parlor speculation, no real discoveries had been documented.

Then in January of 1849 came the word that placer gold had been discovered by James Marshall in California. Opportunistic reporters copied each others' dispatches, sending thousands of would-be Argonauts to the Pacific Coast. They traveled on the Santa Fe, Oregon and a few other minor trails. Some who had the price went by sea. However, as in all rushes, less than ten per cent found gold. The others returned home empty handed. It was one of those unlucky ones who located the yellow metal in what was then western Kansas. His name was William Green Russell and he was returning to his home in Georgia after nine unproductive years spent searching for riches along California's Mother Lode. The year was 1858.

Along the way Russell checked out many western waterways, still hoping to make a find. In present southwest Denver, near the junction of Little Dry Creek with the South Platte River, he found it. It wasn't much, just a few hundred dollars worth of loose gold, but other eastbound travelers spread the story. Soon word of the "Russell Bonanza" reached the East where our national economy was still reeling from the aftershocks of the Panic of 1857. The result was another rush westward. In 1861 western Kansas was made a part of the new Colorado Territory. Two years earlier a rich discovery was made above North Clear Creek in present Gilpin County. What grew up around it came to be known as "The Richest Square Mile On Earth."

In May of 1859 another Georgian, John H. Gregory, red haired and profane, found lode gold in Prosser Gulch above the valley of North Clear Creek. Although Gregory tried at first to suppress the story, the "secret" leaked out by June, and a tumultuous exodus to the hills nearly depopulated little Denver City and Auraria. A small community called Mountain City mushroomed in the narrow confines of the gulch around Gregory's discovery. As for Gregory,

he sold his mine for $21,000 and went to work prospecting for others at $200 a day. Probably because the area was heavily mineralized, many of his locations became paying mines, thereby enhancing his reputation. But Gregory was smart, he thought it over, gave it all up and returned to Georgia with a tidy sum put away for the future. He never returned to Colorado.

Many well known people, among them Mark Twain, came out to see what it was all about. Scrupulously honest Horace Greeley arrived to write a first hand account. When the story appeared in the dispatches to his *New York Tribune* the rush was really on. By the end of June an estimated 10,000 men had found their way up to what was now being called Gregory Gulch.

Others came too, and a few were women. These were people who would never swing a pick, wet a pan nor retort an ounce of ore. They were the land speculators, town boomers, lawyers, confidence men and hard eyed harlots. And of course there were the whiskey sellers who arrived with only a tent, some tin cups, two barrels and a rough plank. These were the only requirements for opening a saloon. They dispensed an incendiary brew from northern New Mexico. It was a crude corn whiskey and they sold it for 50c a cup. Those miners who consumed it insisted that it was a libation of great authority and they dubbed it "Taos Lightning." Its devotees said that after one had swallowed two cups of the stuff the sensation was akin to being struck by a bolt of lightning.

The burgeoning population needed living accommodations that were more adequate than the tents and brush-covered caves that had sheltered the first to arrive. And soon clusters of cabins and frame homes began to form a network of little towns. The first ones appeared in the gulch above and below Mountain City. One visiting journalist described the arrangement of towns as resembling the rungs of a ladder, merging with one another along the steep three miles or so of Gregory Gulch.

At the lower end of the defile was Black Hawk, which had plenty of water but no mines. So it became the refining center. Here several mills lined the banks of Clear Creek. One of these was the great Boston and Colorado Smelter of Nathaniel P. Hill which gained a reputation for squeezing more of the precious metals from Colorado's refractory ores. Later, Hill moved his smelter down to Globeville and embarked upon a political career that put him in the U.S. Senate.

The Richest Square Mile On Earth

by Robert L. Brown

The foreground structures in this photograph are
the community of Mountain City. Central City
appears in the middle distance. The view illustrates
how the towns blended into each other.

Evelyn and Robert L. Brown Collection

Still using the newsman's analogy, the next rung of the ladder was slightly up the hill from Black Hawk. It was a tiny settlement called Gregory Point, a suburb of Mountain City. By mid June these two communities sported more than a hundred buildings, each clinging tenaciously to the steep southern slope of the gulch. There were physicians, a couple of hotels, a printing shop, stores, gambling halls and the inevitable saloons.

Continuing up the gulch, the same reporter said that the towns blended into each other, making it nearly impossible to determine where one ended and the next began. Older residents still insist that no formal boundary ever separated Mountain City from Central City. The latter was easily the largest and most important of the hamlets in the "Richest Square Mile On Earth." Soon another name gained in popularity: the "Little Kingdom of Gilpin."

Down in Black Hawk the main road that bisects the town is known as Gregory Street. Further up the hill it veers off to the left and the main road assumes the name of Lawrence Street, but only for a few blocks. Above the junction with Main Street it becomes Eureka Street because it once extended into the next town, a short lived hamlet known as Eureka. The previously mentioned Main Street is short too. It splits to become Spring Street which leads to Russell Gulch and the site of Springfield. The other branch of the split is Nevada Street. It leads up another hill to Bald Mountain or Nevadaville.

Russell Gulch, two miles from Central City, was the location of a later placer gold discovery by Green Russell. About 1,000 people lived there. In later years the mines produced some $35,000 a week. Russell Gulch was a family town, a quieter place as mining towns go. Until it collapsed in the early 60s, a large Methodist church stood on the steep hillside above the town. Nearby were two more obscure settlements called Bortonsburg and Gilson Gulch.

About 6,000 people lived and worked at Nevadaville and it was a rougher place than Russell Gulch. One end of the town was peopled by Cornish families, fine stoneworkers and superb miners from Cornwall. They were a sturdy, religious people of Celtic origin who were much given to singing and to picturesque beliefs that included Tommyknockers, "little people" who allegedly were found in underground tunnels. Tommyknockers were prone to issue warnings of impending disasters to those who believed and would listen.

At the opposite end of Nevadaville lived the Irish majority who competed with Cornishmen for the same jobs. There are few factors that build animosity like separation and economic competition. Each weekend the Irish-Cornish feud erupted into bloody brawls. Nevadaville's many saloons provided arenas for these "Donnybrooks," but any open space would suffice. Ultimately the two groups banded together to protect themselves when Chinese and central European miners appeared on the scene.

ABOVE: This 1984 photograph shows how little Black Hawk has changed. More than half its buildings are original.

BELOW: Black Hawk's church and school are seen on the hillside above Gregory Street. At far left the street winds uphill to Mountain City. Chase Gulch, at far right, led up to Pat Casey's mine.

Evelyn and Robert L. Brown Collection

ABOVE: Although the growth of trees obscures some of the landmarks, many features of the older view are still evident.

BELOW: A work crew of the Colorado Central Railroad is seen in the foreground. Note the load of ties behind the engine. In the background is early Central City with the Teller House looming above Eureka Street. St. Aloysius Academy is visible on the hill above the city.

Nancy and Ed Bathke Collection

Because there are several other western towns with the same or similar names, Nevada City for instance, delivery of mail was awkward. So the postal authorities called the Nevadaville facility "Bald Mountain." To simplify matters, an effort was made to change the town's name to conform to the postal designation. But the residents braced their feet, refusing to get into line for "Big Brother". The postal laddies proved to be equally stubborn. So the Post Office continued to be called Bald Mountain to the end of its days, while the town retained the name of Nevadaville.

57

ABOVE: This early morning picture was made from the same angle, just after the streets were washed. Note the same buildings in each picture.

BELOW: This early photograph shows a funeral procession at the door of St. James Methodist Church in Central City. The opera house and Teller House are at the right.

The rich Burroughs Lode was unearthed in 1859. Its production continued for many years and supported a number of Nevadaville families. On Quartz Hill above the town stood the rich Casey Mine, another mainstay in the town's economy. It was the property of an itinerant Irishman named Patrick Casey whose eccentric behavior and capacity for liquor became the basis of much Gilpin County folklore. Nevadaville burned three times, and most of its population left early in the present century when the wells dried up.

All of the previously mentioned towns were satellite "bedroom communities" which grew up around the nucleus that was Central City. In common with most of its neighbors, it too began in that magic year 1859. In its best years, about 5,000 people lived and worked there. It became the business, financial and recreation center of the district, and is still the county seat. It has been estimated that a ratio of five workers prevailed to support each miner. In other words it required five non-miners working above ground to provide the needed services that kept each hardrock miner underground. In Central City these service people included restaurant men, haberdashers, stablers, grocers, saloon keepers and a host of others. A railroad, the Colorado Central, laid its tracks up Clear Creek Canyon from Golden to Black Hawk, then up twisting Gregory Gulch to 8,500 foot high Central City. Later a spur line was constructed

east to Denver. Poorly paid Chinese workers put down the tracks and ties. The first train ran from Denver to Black Hawk on December 15, 1872. Although Central City is less than a mile above Black Hawk, some 500 feet of elevation separate the two towns. More than three miles of looping tracks and trestles were needed to make the connection. The first locomotive steamed into Central City on May 2, 1878. With the decline in the worth of gold, rail service was discontinued in 1931.

By 1872 the plush Teller House hotel had opened its doors to the public. It was named to honor Henry M. Teller, one of Colorado's first two U.S. Senators. Later, President Arthur made him Secretary of the Interior. Teller made his money in mining and railroading, but by profession he was a Central City attorney. To enhance the cultural attributes of the city, an Opera House was built in 1878. It attracted a variety of itinerant theatrical companies, jugglers, acrobats and an occasional opera company. In 1874 a fire swept away much of the city, excluding only masonry structures like the Teller House. Native stone, brick and masonry buildings gradually replaced the destroyed wooden ones.

Even U.S. Grant visited Central City, both as a General and later as President. Supposedly, he and Mrs. Grant entered the Teller House by walking across a walkway of solid silver bricks made available for the occasion by Nathaniel Hill's Boston and Colorado Smelter down at Black Hawk. What a

ABOVE: Contemporary Main Street still retains much of its pioneer flavor. Note the same house on the hill in the middle distance.

BELOW: This view shows a parade on Central City's Main Street. Note the absence of spectators in the grandstand at the left. Were they all in the parade?

Evelyn and Robert L. Brown Collection

ABOVE: This contemporary view was taken in 1978. It shows all of the churches and many of the other landmarks that make Central City worth a visit.

BELOW: Here was Central City in 1885. A baseball field appears at lower left. The blur to its right is a train pulling into the station. The Armory, with its roof under construction, is at the center. The Methodist, Episcopal, and Catholic churches all show in this view.

stroke of irony that ingots of silver were used in a town whose fortunes were based upon gold. Eastern reporters, never blind to a useful publicity stunt, spread the story that Colorado was so rich that even the sidewalks were paved with silver and that President Grant had walked upon such a sidewalk.

With that, the final eastern doubts vanished and a new little rush of people was underway. In all a half billion dollars came out of the ''Richest Square Mile On Earth,'' a statistic that becomes more meaningful

Gilpin County Historical Society Collection

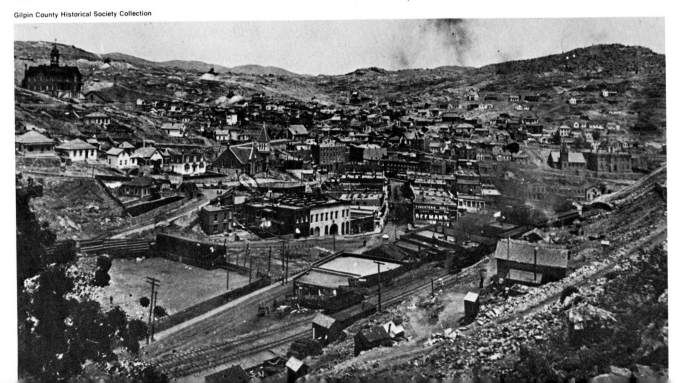

Evelyn and Robert L. Brown Collection

when we remember that the price of gold was then only $20 an ounce. When Colorado became a state in 1876 Central City was briefly considered as the capital. Some years ago Hollywood discovered the town and several productions have been filmed there, but tourism is now the cornerstone of its economy. Today most of Central City remains, lovingly preserved to reflect its unique mining heritage.

ABOVE: Although the mountain profile remains unchanged, three fires have nearly destroyed Nevadaville.

BELOW: Nevadaville, the Irish-Cornish town, is less than a mile above Central City. This photograph looks down on the town from Quartz Hill.

Fred and Jo Mazzula Collection

came into existence during the summer of 1933 when my builder, Max Gordon, decided to live here next to his little "Last Chance" mine. I was not here at all, of course, when Max first discovered silver in the hill behind my foundations, but I can at least put together some thoughts on the subject from conversations I have heard between Max and his friends. Max was alone and quiet during most of the twenty years he spent here, but he did have partners, on occasion, to help with the mine.

Max may have preferred to be away from other people, but he was never really alone here, for we formed a very close and intimate relationship over the years. We were the best of friends and shared our liking for the great pine forest where we lived in harmony with the chipmunks, squirrels, birds and other wildlife. I believe Max must have had great difficulty living within the society of people in the cities during the so-called depression days, and found that he could be adequately comfortable here, making enough money from the Last Chance to live on. He never really spent much time working in the mine, only as much as he found necessary in order to make his living. He would much rather work with rocks in building neat walls, foundations and walkways, or on projects for his own relaxation—like the hammock he fashioned out of a wooden barrel. One day he had some friends help him lift a huge flat boulder atop two others to form what he called "The dangdest, heaviest picnic table in the world".

As for my own construction, I was built of whole pine logs, flattened on the inside with a broad-ax. My roof was flat with rough-cut boards layed on log rafters, and I measured ten by twenty feet in size. I had a small window at each end and a somewhat larger one on the front, facing east, as did the doorway, facing toward a view of Squaw and Chief Mountains. Max installed a large wood-burning kitchen stove in my northwest corner, a few shelves, a small table and a bed. On my north side, where Cascade Creek flowed nearby, an outside cabinet was attached to my wall for storage of food which needed to be kept cool.

Max loved to build anything he could out of available materials to make us both more comfortable. Outside, he laid flat stones along all the pathways, one going all the way down the hill to the spring. Max was very pleased with the natural spring, because it would always supply clean, fresh water, even late in the season after Cascade Creek dried up. The stream itself was very beautiful in spring and early summer. During snow melt run-off, it would overflow its banks and run down the road. The path from the road crossed the stream on a neat wooden bridge which had a railing made of aspen wood. This bridge was also the route to the corrugated iron outhouse and the woodshed. Max spent more time, I believe, in cutting firewood for the stove than anything else.

We had a delightful relationship over the years, with Max keeping his lonely schedule of an hour or two of digging in the mine each day, firewood cutting, stone laying and tending to his two jacks whose names were "Jessica" and "Ned." Max used the jacks to haul in supplies and to take the sacks of ore from the mine into Georgetown, two miles over the hill to the west.

The late afternoons and evenings were spent in much thought, I suppose, for Max would spend many hours just sitting on the porch by my door, smoking his pipe and gazing out across the Chicago Creek valley. On quiet evenings we could hear the buzzing and crackling of the high power line which came over the hill a few hundred feet to the south. The power line was built back in 1915 to carry electricity from the Shoshone Power Plant in Glenwood Canyon to Denver. That was one of the first such lines to be built in the country, and it crossed the continental divide three times along the way. The buzzing sound was particularly loud on foggy and snowy days when the moisture in the air caused corona discharge off the wires which carried 150,000 volts.

One visitor, who came to see us about once every month, was Les Thompson, who worked for the Public Service Company of Colorado as highline inspector. His job was to keep a constant watch on the line for any troubles that might exist. He occasionally brought Max pieces of old cable, used insulators and other discarded parts from the power line that were not needed. Max always liked to save "junk" like this and would promptly store it away in the shed near the mine.

I always dreaded the coming of late fall because I knew that the on-coming winter would make it necessary for Max to leave me until the following spring. He would always hang on as long as he could, until late November usually, when the snow began to get too deep. He would then pack up the jacks with his personal things and a last load of ore before heading for Georgetown, where he spent the winter. Max often seemed to use the jacks to take out his verbal frustrations, something he never did with me. Each time he left, I could hear him talking in his accented, gruff voice to them. It seemed that Jessica always caught it more than Ned, for she was blind and had trouble, stumbling and running into trees. I'd often hear Max saying something like, "Jessica, you gol-danged blind old son-of-a-gun, cain't ya see where you're goin'?" The loneliness of winter would then close in, but being a cabin, I was built to have patience.

Spring would finally come and Cascade Creek would swell with foaming water from the melting snows. Sure enough, far back in the forest, I would hear Max calling to his jacks as they returned for the season, loaded down with provisions.

Max was obviously getting old, and, during his last few years here, would come later in the spring and leave earlier in the fall. He made his last trek up here in early summer of 1952, after all the snow had melted. He had only Ned with him this time, as Jessica had apparently died. Max only stayed about

Reflections Of

a month, and did no work to speak of, but spent most of his time in deep thought, as if going over the many good years we had spent together. As indicated by the calendar on my wall, he left during July, 1952, and never returned. I remember well that day when Max carried his few belongings out to Ned and came back to sit on my porch for over an hour, gazing away toward Squaw Mountain. He finally got up very slowly, shut my door then headed for Ned and walked through the woods toward Georgetown. I waited patiently all that summer and fall thinking, ''Max has left me. I wonder if he will ever return?''

The only other person I saw that summer was Les, who stopped one day to look for Max. He had a coil of power line wire for him which he placed inside the shed before he went back to his power line work. The way Les looked at me before he left indicated that he must have known Max might not be back.

By the time fall came and the aspen leaves had turned gold, I was beginning to get used to existing alone. I wasn't really alone, of course, because my friends the pack-rats still lived under my floor and would now spend even more time scampering about my interior searching for materials to build their nests. The birds perched on my roof, as always, using me for a favorite lookout point. A couple of times I saw a jeep or truck working its way up the road toward Highland Park, but no one came up my road to visit me. I was not visible from the main road and most people didn't realize I was here. The snows finally came, bringing with them the peaceful, quiet season I was used to. The rodents would go into semi-hibernation, but the birds would continue to gather on my roof. Occasionally I would see deer, rabbits, bobcats and coyotes wander by, but they seemed ever-cautious and kept their distance.

Les came by on his snowshoes one day when the weather was very cold and windy. For the first time since Max had left he came inside to get warm, building a small fire in the stove before continuing his hike over to Georgetown. This became a habit with him over the next few years when the weather was bad.

During the summer of 1953, a few people came by in their jeeps, coming inside to look about with curiosity. They were friendly enough and obviously wondered who might have built and lived in me. They would then carefully close my door and continue on up the road.

In the fall of that year I recognized some of the same people who had visited during the summer. This time they came inside prepared to spend the night. These men were obviously here for deer hunting, since they had their rifles with them. I knew this was the time of year for hunting, since Max would bring home deer he had shot about the time the aspen were turning yellow. Max once brought home a large buck, and was so proud of it, he mounted the antlers on the front of my roof, an ornament that stayed with me as long as I existed. The hunters that stayed here this time were friendly enough, but somehow the intimate feeling that

''Max''

Drawings by Nancy Lee Smith

always existed between me and Max was lacking. They stayed three days and had no luck with their hunting as Max always did. My only other visitor that winter was Les, who stopped by twice to warm

During the long winter I often felt the weight of the heavy snow bearing down on my roof and my rafters would creak under the heavy load. On warm days the snow would melt and run toward the back of the roof, soaking the logs of the back wall and drip water through holes in the roof to wet the interior floor.

Several years went by with only an occasional visitor, other than Les, and the same hunters, who seemed to enjoy returning each season. During the five years they came to hunt, they were successful in getting only two deer, but they always seemed to enjoy the stay.

The last ten winters had been relatively mild when compared with those of the 1930s and first few years of the 1940s, but one day in the spring of 1957 an unusually heavy, wet snow came. This was finally more than I could take. Three of my rotting rafters broke under the weight and my roof sagged inward at a steep angle. This allowed more melting snow and rain to run inside to cover the walls and floor of my south end. The dampness allowed fungus to grow on the inside of my ceiling. I really longed for the days when Max took such good care of me.

A Mountain Cabin

by Ron Ruhoff

Ron Ruhoff at the cabin in 1958.

One early June day in 1957 I heard my first visitors of the season coming up the road. Two boys of about eighteen were driving an old, faded green jeep which had its windshield laying flat on the hood. They came up the road as far as they could until a large snowdrift stopped them from reaching the bridge. They seemed very excited about being here and I heard one exclaim loudly, "Hey, Ralph, look! A cabin!" Of all the people who had come by here since Max left, I had never seen anyone so happy to see me as Ralph's friend Ron. I didn't know it at the time, but a new relationship was opening, one that would turn out to be the happiest of my existence. Ralph and Ron didn't stay long that day, but they certainly looked me and the mine over thoroughly before leaving. Ron mentioned something about being sorry his camera was out of film, because he sure wanted to take a picture of me. I had no idea what he meant at the time, but would learn later from Ron what photography was all about. When Ralph and Ron left that day, I had a feeling they would be back before long.

Actually, it was about a month before Ron returned, this time with a friend named John. They came late in the afternoon of a July day, driving the same old jeep. I knew they intended to spend the night inside me because they carried a camp stove and sleeping bags. Once inside, they looked around sadly at the mess which had accumulated on my floor. I was cluttered with old newspapers and

magazines which Max had left behind and which the pack-rats had shredded and strewn about. They started right off cleaning me up. John got a fire going in the stove while Ron found Max's old broom and swept the floor. He piled the magazines in the corner, and threw all the cans and trash out the door into the pit where Max had been throwing his trash. Ron then found the kerosene lamp, or what was left of it. The rats had knocked it over and broken the glass bowl which held the oil, but the wick holder and chimney had survived. He then located the kerosene can in the cabinet and filled a coffee cup with it and placed the wick and chimney on top so the wick would dip into the oil. Sure enough, the lamp lit and burned brightly as new.

John and Ron talked about me while eating their dinner, wondering who lived here and when I was built. They noticed the 1952 calendar on the wall and guessed correctly that the owner must have left that year. Ron seemed very enthused about finding out who owned me and wondered if he might be able to buy me for his own use. After they finished dinner, they cleared a place on my floor for their sleeping bags and spent a comfortable night. I felt good that night, for I knew I was sheltering some people who seemed to care for me.

It was Ron who returned several times that year, each time with different friends, but always filled with enthusiasm about me. Each time they came they would throw more trash into the pit and sweep my floor of the mess left by the pack rats.

I learned a lot more about the area where I was located from listening to Ron talk with his friends. He had explored all the roads in the area by now and loved to see where each one led. I learned that it was possible to drive a jeep in here by a number of different routes other than the usual way through the old ghost town of Lamartine. One could follow the Cascade Creek road all the way from Chicago Creek, or come over the hill from Lawson. Lamartine was a favorite subject of Ron's since it was the first ghost town he ever visited. The little mining town had about 500 people living in it around the turn of the century. They worked the large Lamartine Mine, which was named after the French poet Alphonse de Lamartine. By the time Max came along in the 1930s, Lamartine was already a ghost town.

Ron continued to come here quite often between 1957 and 1961 with many different friends. We always had a good time together and more clean up work was done each time. Considerable amounts of trash were burned in the pit and other junk was hauled to an old mineshaft near Lamartine. Bob and Margaret Swanlund, who operated the fire lookout atop Squaw Mountain, were always notified so they would know the origin of the smoke.

Ron commented that he still had not found my original owner. If only I could talk, I could have told him about Max myself. I often wondered if Max were still living. These mysteries were finally cleared up in 1961, when Mrs. Johnson, of the Clear Creek County assayer's office in Georgetown, found my owner by using a photograph given to her by Ron. It turned out that Max was still living in Georgetown. Ron went to meet him and found him living in a very small home with boarded up windows near the north end of town. He told Ron, briefly, his story about me and the Last Chance Mine and said he would sell the claim and cabin via a ''quit claim deed'' for $100. Ron bought the claim and learned from the county office that it was an unpatented mine and that he would have to do assessment work on the property each year. As it turned out, Ron met Max only that one time, as he was very old and passed away shortly thereafter. I often have the feeling that Max has somehow returned here and is happy to be home—a place to remain always.

I now had a new owner and spent the winter of 1961-1962 waiting in excitement to see what the following summer would bring. Ron obviously had nice plans for me, for he drove up here early in the spring in a brand new green jeep and immediately came inside with notepad and tape measure to begin planning for repairs. A bit later in the summer he returned in a pickup truck loaded down with boards and sheet aluminum. His friend Glen Sprague was behind him driving the green jeep. It was nearly dark when they arrived, so they saved the unloading for the next day. I remember well the tremendous steaks they brought for their dinner that evening. Ron built a fire of aspen wood in the stove, explaining to Glen that this was the best way to broil steaks because of the wonderful flavor. Glen had never tasted aspen cooking and was a bit doubtful of Ron's claims. When the steaks were ready to eat, Glen said, ''Where's the salt?'' They looked all around, but could find none. Glen was really upset and said, ''I can't eat steak without salt!''

Ron said, ''Glen, with aspen cooking, you don't need salt, because the wood adds a lot of flavor.'' Glen was pleasantly surprised, but still grumbled about the missing salt, an incident he never let Ron forget.

Next day more help arrived as Bob Wintersteen, Bill Dwinelle and Bill Wright drove up to help with the new roof. The day was beautiful and they got to work right away tearing my old roof completely off and replacing it with new 2x8 rafters covered with 1 inch boards and sheets of corrugated aluminum roofing. I then got a new little pot-bellied stove, which Bill Wright had sold to Ron, and a new smokestack to go with it. This stove was installed in the center of my room near the back wall, and the old broken kitchen stove was discarded into the pit. By the end of the day the roof was complete except for the fill-in between rafters. Bob Wintersteen donated a nice studio couch which he had purchased at an auction for 50 cents. Everyone but Ron and Glen had to get back home that evening, but not until all had their fill of aspen cooked hamburgers and Coors Beer. If I could have talked myself, I would have given everyone much thanks for helping build my new roof, but Ron made up for it and offered the use of me whenever anyone wanted to come.

The next day saw the completion of rafter fill and a brand new, larger door. When Ron and Glen finally left at the end of the day, I stood there swelled to the top of my new smokestack with pride and happiness. They had re-mounted Max's deer antlers nice and straight on the front of my roof. Max would have been proud too, I'm sure, if he could only have seen me that day. Ron had even put up signs at the crossroads below the bridge to indicate my address—''WEST 48th, PLUMB''—meaning I was 48 miles from Denver and plumb back in the sticks!

In October Ron made his last trip here for the year, this time with friends Ron and JoAnn Luke. They completed the job of installing new windows and

"One early June day in 1957 I heard my first visitors of the season coming up the road. Two boys of about eighteen were driving an old, faded green Jeep which had its windshield laying flat on the hood."

placed a lock on the door. My inside was now neat as a pin. Max's original table and chairs were still in use and the new 50 cent couch completed the list of furniture. A new broom stood in the corner and the cabinet shelves were stocked with useful items like matches, lamp oil, teapot, saucepan, tea bags, coffee, soap, single-burner Coleman stove and salt — just in case Glen cooked another steak. A new kerosene lamp sat on the table, and a portable kerosene lamp hung from the ceiling. For the first time in many years I was completely dry inside.

Les came by for the last time late that fall while checking the highline. Ron had talked to Les by phone and had learned that the Public Service Company was turning to helicopter reconnaissance of their power lines instead of the old method of walking, and Les's job was now over. Ron had told Les of the hiding place for the cabin key in case he wanted to come for shelter, but Les came by only one more time, and didn't come in. He just stood and looked at me for a long time, much as he had done when Max had finally left for good. I believe Les was going to miss his job of walking the line.

The years 1963 through 1966 were happy times for me. I was kept clean and Ron brought many good friends here to visit, and, on occasion, some of these friends would come on their own to spend some time. I would now like to relate a few stories from those beautiful years.

Ron and his friends were not my only companions, for I also enjoyed the many species of wildlife who lived here in the forest. Ron loved them too and often made good friends of them. The pack rats lived within my foundations as did many species of spiders and insects. The larger animals like deer, elk, fox, skunks, raccoons, bobcats, porcupines and coyotes were always around, but Ron rarely, if ever, saw them himself. He knew they were about from reading their tracks and he often heard the coyotes

howl in the distance. The coyote family that lived over near the highline would howl in chorus at times, making a thrilling sound. Ron worked during the night at the phone company in Denver and would often come up here to rest during the day, then leave about 10 PM to go back to work. One night as Ron was leaving, he stood for a moment in the doorway and howled like a coyote. Much to his surprise the whole coyote family answered in chorus. What a beautiful way to say "goodnight" to his forest friends as he got in his jeep and headed for Denver.

Of the many species of birds who lived here, the gray jay or "campbird" was the most friendly. The chickadees and humming birds would come around close to feed, and the owls would hoot from nearby trees at night, but the campbirds were real companions. They loved to ask for food treats and became so friendly they would often come right inside to sit on the table next to Ron's plate to ask for their handouts. They would cock their heads, make cooing sounds, and look up into Ron's face with an expression that would all but allow them to talk English. Ron learned to recognize their amazing variety of sounds in relation to what they were saying. One day Ron left a whole, large biscuit on the table, figuring it would keep them busy for awhile. He was surprised to see one campbird grab the whole thing, take off with some difficulty and fly away with it. He was sure the bird was laughing at the time.

Ron often sat on the doorstep, as Max used to, enjoying the view of Squaw Mountain to the east. At these times, the chipmunks and ground squirrels would happily take handouts from his hand.

The pack rats were a real nuisance and Ron finally decided that he would have to get rid of them. They would constantly chew on bedding, food containers and even my floorboards. They are also known as "trade rats" because of their habit of swapping what might be in their mouths for a shiny item that looked better. One day Ron had just cleaned off the table completely and walked over to get the broom to sweep the floor. He heard a noise and looked back to find an old corncob right in the middle of the table where nothing had been moments before. He knew right away who the little trickster was and couldn't help but wonder what it had taken in place of the corncob. Nothing of importance was missing however. After this incident Ron was prompted to place rat poison under the floor and the pests were finally eliminated.

Ron, unlike most other people, never found spiders to be particularly objectionable. They were not like regular insects, and were really little house-keepers in their own way. Their webs would have to be cleaned out occasionally, but they did catch flies and other annoying bugs. Spiders vary a lot in appearance, some being quite ugly, but others had more friendly faces and could look up with eight shiny little eyes as if to say "thanks" for a nice place to live.

Ron introduced me to a new and delightful sound called "music" by way of a battery powered radio he often brought along. These sounds often reminded me of those with which I was already familiar, like the rippling of the stream, the bird and coyote sounds, the patter of rain and rumble of thunder, the wind blowing through the tall trees and the hum and buzz of insects. I believe that these natural sounds must have given early people the original ideas for their music as they attempted to imitate what they heard on various instruments. Some of the pieces played on Ron's radio directly refered to such natural sounds like Respighi's "The Birds", "Mysterious Mountain" by Hovhaness, "An Alpine Symphony" by Strauss and "Flight of the Bumblebee" by Rimsky-Korsakov.

One day Ron was working outside and had the radio on the outer windowsill playing "La Mer" by Debussy. At the same time fluffy clouds were rolling by in time with the music and looked much like great waves in the sea. When the music came to the part depicting a storm, the clouds overhead responded and built up to thunderheads with rain. Ron brought the radio inside just in time for a real thunderstorm. The music continued to follow in time, making a very beautiful experience.

Late one day during the winter of 1964-65, I heard music drifting through the woods below me. It was Ron, coming in on snowshoes with a tremendous backpack and his beloved radio playing away inside it. He had hiked up from Cascade Creek, a distance of four miles from where he had parked the jeep. This was the first time anyone had come to spend the night within me during the winter. Ron didn't realize it at the time, but, according to the tracks he found in the snow the next day, he had been followed for nearly a mile by a bobcat. Once inside Ron set about building a fire and lighting the lamp. The outside temperature was only three degrees that night, but he was warm and comfortable on the couch for the night.

Next morning Ron snowshoed all the way up the hill to the Comet Mine shaft at Highland Park, where one can drive a jeep in the summer and view Silver Plume and Georgetown far below. He was surprised to have several chickadees follow him all the way up

and back again, asking for handouts all the way.

Late in the afternoon Ron packed up and headed on down the trail on the snowshoes, radio playing strains of Brahms Symphony No. 3 along the way as swirling snowflakes from a new storm softly swallowed his tracks.

A forest ranger came by one day in June, 1966 and, after looking me and the mine over thoroughly, left a note on my door. When Ron found the note, he read, "Would like to know status of this mine and property. Thank you, Dave White, U.S.F.S. Idaho Springs."

I heard Ron discussing the note with friends and it seemed that we were having trouble because of the fact that this mine property was not patented. Ron had been turning in the required affidavit of improvements each year, but the forest service was now cracking down on those who were using invalid and un-patented claims for cabin sites. Ron spent much time with the forest people, but finally came to the conclusion that nothing could be done about it since our mine offered little hope of showing any value to the government inspectors.

During the summer of 1965, Ron bought a new cabin near Evergreen in a spot called Pine Valley, and moved there from his Denver home. We continued to have good times together until the fall of 1966 when we finally had to say goodbye. After finding no way to get around the forest service rules, Ron signed me over to them so they could burn me down, re-claim the twenty acre lode claim, and return it to forest service status. Ron made a final visit here in October, 1966, to take home what he could use from my furnishings. He loaded his new Bronco with my front door, the windows, the little stove, the antlers from the roof and various smaller things stored inside. He thought about taking the studio couch, but not having enough room for it, decided it had more than fulfilled its fifty cent price and would leave it behind. Ron looked at me for a long time before driving away. It was a difficult parting, but, at least, we understood each other.

I had the whole winter of 1966-67 to think about my fate, for the rangers never did show up that fall to set me afire as they had planned. I gave much thought to my thirty-four years of existence and owners Max and Ron. We had shared years of beautiful times together, and I had provided shelter to many friends. A new era was beginning which was filling with a breed of people who seemed to actually

The town of Lamartine, Colorado. The photograph was taken circa 1900.

enjoy destroying things. More and more of these destructive people were penetrating the mountains in their many varieties of back-country vehicles, and I was in constant danger of vandalism. Ron seemed to feel that it was probably just as well that I be destroyed in the manner which the forest service intended, so that the wrong kind of people could not get to me. He wanted to always remember me as I had been during those good years, and he would use the stove and other items salvaged from me in his new cabin to provide a kind of continuance of our friendship.

In May, 1967, the rangers finally came, and, without hesitation, poured kerosene on my floors and walls and set fire to me. I had dreaded the coming of this moment, but found that as I burned, I was as aware as ever. As my walls crumbled and the intense heat melted my roof into molten blobs of aluminum, I found that a feeling of relaxing contentment came over me because I knew I had served my purpose well and had made many people warm and happy. I was also glad to know that I would never become the target of those who would wish to use me for target practice or other form of destructive mischief.

When all was burned and the rangers were satisfied that no harm would come to the forest from the fire, they left. I was somewhat surprised to realize that, although I was physically gone, I remained, as always in my beloved forest, a conscience presence. I now understood that this ''presence'' is kept intact by the thoughts of the many people who have known me, both those alive and those gone beyond like Max. The many photographs which Ron took of me will also provide a continued reference to my appearance. My continued contentment, I know, is a reflection of the fond memories so many people retain of our good times together.

Ron continues to come by occasionally to enjoy this beautiful location and to reminisce about past days here. He always takes the time to sit for awhile on my stone porch and gaze out toward Squaw Mountain. I believe he can still imagine that I am right behind him as before. At times like this, we communicate, we understand, we share the smell of pine, aspen and wind, the ripple of Cascade Creek, the drifting clouds, our animal friends and, above all, we are happy.

68

Ron Ruhoff Photograph

Glen and Ron eat their steaks in this view of the cabin interior.

"Ron had even put up signs at the crossroads below the bridge to indicate my address - 'West 48th, Plumb' - meaning I was 48 miles from Denver, and plumb back in the sticks."

Ron Ruhoff Photograph

The sky was a brilliant blue, aspen, aglow with their finest golden jewelry, shimmered in the fall sunlight. Scampering to and fro, squirrels made preparation for their winter retreat. Cattle ambled aimlessly over the yellowing pastures in seeming anticipation of the move to lower altitude. A whisper of a breeze rustled pastel brown oak leaves gently, and in the distance the haunting sound of a steam locomotive whistle reverberated plaintively off the surrounding hillsides.

The sound of the oncoming train, though muted and mellowed by the rolling hills adjacent to Wolf Creek, became much sharper and distinct as it continued its assault on the four percent grade of Cumbres Pass. The first glimpse of the narrow gauge train came when its locomotive, belching smoke and billowing steam, rounded a small hill; followed by its charge of diminutive freight cars. Another steam locomotive appeared, sandwiched amid the freight cars, pushing some of the cars ahead and pulling those behind it. With the passing of the caboose, the click-clack sound of steel wheels on steel rails faded away into the past.

During the time it had taken for the train to pass, the viewer was convinced that the calendar had been turned back to the early 1950s. The scenario repeated itself a number of times along the grade as the train churned laboriously toward the summit of the pass. A narrow gauge freight train powered by steam locomotives in the mountains of southwest Colorado and northwest New Mexico had been a regular event thirty years ago. Flat cars and gondola cars equipped to haul pipe to the oil fields of the San Juan basin, and the markings of the locomotives and freight cars (the flying *Rio Grande* herald of the Denver & Rio Grande Railroad) gave evidence of a bygone era.

There are two tunnels on the C&TS railroad, located 4 miles apart at the eastern end of Toltec Gorge. As engine 482 emerged from the western bore, the fireman of engine 481 gazed down an almost-perpendicular rocky cliff to the bottom of the chasm about 600 feet below.

When the train at last ground to a halt in the cinder packed yard at Cumbres, the mid-train helper locomotive was switched out, turned on the snow-shed covered wye track, and returned to the engine terminal at Chama. The freight train then resumed its eastward journey after being reassembled.

During the 1950s, scenes such as those just described were so common that scarcely anyone paid much attention to them. However, this particular train's operation occurred in early October of 1983 and was the culmination of many painstaking hours of planning and organization on the part of Bill and Mary Ann Peter, the cooperation of the management and employees of the Cumbres & Toltec Scenic Railroad, and the desires and dreams of approximately sixty devoted narrow gauge rail fans.

Bill and Mary Ann, who own and operate a model railroad business in Chama, New Mexico, first proposed the idea of the special railroad experience to the management of the Cumbres & Toltec. Then, with the railroad's approval of the idea, narrow gauge railfans were contacted to determine their specific interests and desires as to what should be included. When all had been finalized, the fans were again contacted and informed of the costs and details. When commitments from the railfans started coming in, organization began in earnest for the feeding, lodging, and transportation of the group. Supplies were purchased for the renovation of the freight cars to be employed.

Late in September fans began arriving in Chama. The group was a diverse one; their professions as different as the locations from which they came. There was a lawyer from Texas, a mechanic from Pennsylvania, a commercial artist from Arizona, from New Mexico came a professional photographer, from Louisiana a retired army officer, a forester from Colorado, a research engineer from California, a tool and die maker, a stock broker, and a beer distributor. Fans from Canada and Scotland added an international flavor to the group. The common bond that brought these fans together was their interest in the narrow gauge railroad and the opportunity to be involved with such a unique train.

The freight cars to be used for the train were checked by the employees of the railroad to assure that the antiquated equipment could be operated safely. Many of the cars were in dire need of external

Yesterday Revisited

by Richard A. Bell

Richard A. Bell Photograph

Richard A. Bell Photograph

ABOVE: C&TS loco-
motives 481 and 482 were
temporarily relettered
"Rio Grande" for this
special nighttime portrait
taken at Chama in 1983.
It's incredible, but these
engines are nearly 60
years old.

C&TS painters have
completed their work on
an ex-D&RGW boxcar,
and are applying the stencils for identification and
safety notices.

Richard A. Bell Photograph

ABOVE: Participating in a 1983 re-enactment of a long-vanished era, C&TS 482 and 481 ascend the 4% grade from Chama toward Cumbres Pass, just over the boundary in Colorado.

BELOW: C&TS 482 and 481, with a long freight train, all relettered in their original designations for a 1983 special trip, are seen here at Windy Point, immediately west of Cumbres Pass.

Richard A. Bell Photograph

restoration. Most had not been utilized since freight operations ceased in the late 1960s. They were moved to a track where the fans could paint and letter them and not interfere with the scheduled operations of the tourist railroad.

A few of the railfans began the restoration process with the fervor of prize winning railroad modelers—which some of them are. The paint was applied with great care on the cars and haphazardly on everything else in the immediate vicinity; including each other. One painter was heard to say, "No pictures of me doing this! Because if my wife sees it I'll have to do the house." The lettering process was diligently pursued. Almost out of nowhere a library of information was assembled from the fans' books and photographs of the equipment as it appeared in the fifties. Lettering diagrams were sketched out, measurements made for exact placement, and stencils found or made to assure proper markings. Each stencil was accurately placed and the paint applied with the diligence of a surgeon.

Other fans worked on the lettering for the locomotives. Artistic license was taken in choosing the locomotive numbers; 482 and 481 were actually locomotives 489 and 487 respectively. All other markings were precisely applied.

The final act of preparation was to sweep years of accumulated dirt and dust from the boxcar interiors. These cars were to be used as bedrooms at Sublette. People who probably never used a broom before were observed leaning out of dust enshrouded boxcar doors attempting to get a breath of fresh air.

In the evening, on the final day of preparation, the group assembled; paint stained and dusty, but otherwise enthusiastic and ready for a night photo session.

Photo line courtesy was observed by all, each checking with the others so as not to appear in some-

Richard A. Bell Photograph

C&TS 482 poses among the aspen trees and the "phantom" rock pillars between the tunnels east of Toltec Gorge.

one else's photo of locomotives at the double spout water tank and the coal tower.

With anticipation levels high, most of the participants arrived at the railroad yards prior to sunrise the next morning. Photographic equipment of every description was ready to record the journey of the double headed freight. Railfans, and many residents of Chama, participated in the eight in the morning departure—a happening that went unnoticed in the fifties. Two locomotives, eighteen freight cars, a bunk car, and a caboose in the company of sixty ardent travelers began the four percent climb to Cumbres.

Along the cottonwood lined banks of Rio Chama, onto Lobato Trestle, the train rolled, encumbered with its load of passengers. Through stands of golden aspen, past Cresco Tank, skirting Hamilton's Point, its whistle howling for the Coxo highway crossing the train swayed on. Steam and coal smoke permeated the air as the train continued its climb snaking around Windy Point and cresting at Cumbres Pass. Then down grade from the 10,015 foot summit, through the broad meadows adjacent to the meandering Rio de Los Pinos, across the spindly appearing Cascade Trestle and onto lonely remnants of the ghost town of Osier, its course guided by two rails. Along the precipitous edge of Toltec Gorge to Garfield Monument, a reminder of past events, into Rock Tunnel and onward to the dramatic rock formations of Phantom Curve, through Mud Tunnel to Sublette, the destination of this nostalgic journey. The locomotive and part of the train proceeded to Big Horn Wye to be turned while most of the fans detrained to prepare dinner and their sparse accommodations for the night.

The morning dawned clear for the return trip, fans prepared for the runbys scheduled at some of the points of interest passed the previous day. Back along the line the train traveled, recorded on the film of the cameras and in the minds of the riders. By journey's end, all were tired, a bit grubby and ready to return to their diverse lives; yet, some suggested that they would like once again to experience yesterday, sometime in the future.

At Coxo siding, west of Cumbres Pass, C&TS 482 runs around its train in the late afternoon of a beautiful fall day.

BELOW: In this unusual scene just east of Los Pinos, C&TS 482 is seen crossing the high steel trestle spanning a deep side canyon at the upper end of Toltec Gorge.

Richard A. Bell Photograph

ABOVE: Through a typically dry mountain valley north of Chama in the fall, C&TS 4-8-2 labors up the 4% grade toward the summit of Cumbres Pass at 10,015 feet.

BELOW: Disguised temporarily as Rio Grande 482, the C&TS engine has halted at Los Pinos tank prior to the final assault on Cumbres Pass. In the background is the La Manga Pass road and the lower level of track.

Stan Zamonski Photograph

Northwest Colorado

Looking for an escape, a shift in the scenery? Trying to get the most out of your vacation? Then head for Northwest Colorado, but be prepared to travel slowly, to really look at what you see. Northwest Colorado is not the place to dash in and dash out. There is much local color here, and it takes time to savor and appreciate it.

This part of Colorado is big in size and variety—larger than the state of Connecticut. It is situated in the heart of the Rockies, with its massive peaks snow-capped the year 'round. It is still a frontier, and much remains of the unspoiled domain of the Native American, trapper and pioneer.

In the last hundred years, little has changed along the rugged Grand Hogback on the road from Rifle to Meeker; well, it's changed a little—it used to take ten hours to make the 42 mile trip, a distance today's traveler can drive in a little over half an hour. Shepherds still carry rifles in scabbards slung from their saddles, and some of the old log cabins still have smoke curling up from their chimneys, but women today in Meeker are more likely to wear sweaters and slacks than long, taffeta dresses.

Here, the many attractions are free, with historic monuments, prehistoric lake beds, petrified woods, Indian rock paintings, and many more wonders.

Meeker is the gateway to the famous Rangley Oil Fields, and this vast region has some of the largest uranium, vanadium and coal deposits in the state. Yet, life is leisurely, with through traffic stopped occasionally by sheep coming down from the high country for winter.

Cowboy hats and boots are still the accustomed garb of the people of Meeker, where livestock and agriculture are the principal source of income. Situated on State Highway 13, almost midway between Rifle and Craig, the town serves the White River Valley, where cattle grow fat on rich native grasses. Sheep were introduced into the region when hard times forced stockmen into new fields, but it took years for the "woolies" to be accepted by the cowboys.

The town was known in its early days as a fishing resort, the country roundabout containing many lakes and trout streams. Today, with a population of roughly three-thousand, Meeker is the county seat and business center for Rio Blanco County.

Meeker gained national recognition as a result of the Meeker Massacre of 1879. The White River Ute Agency was located ten miles from the present town of Meeker. Nathaniel C. Meeker was appointed agent in 1878. He knew very little about Indians and was a starry eyed idealist (formerly a newspaper editor and writer). He arrived determined to make farmers out of the Utes.

The twelve million acre reservation was a peaceful area, with broad meadows and rushing streams which were filled with fish. The Indians lived by hunting, and by trading furs and horses. This was augmented with a small annuity from the federal government. Meeker, in his desire to bring agriculture to the natives, had men plow up the Ute grazing land and their horse racing track. The action infuriated the Utes.

In the spring of 1879 a band of angry Utes stole stock, burned houses and started fires in the area. Meeker became alarmed and asked for military protection; however, the troops were defeated by the Utes, who the same day attacked the agency at White River killing Meeker and the men who were there. The women and children were carried off, and all the buildings were burned.

When additional military aid arrived the Indians scattered. It took the intervention of Chief Ouray to convince the Utes to end what undoubtedly would have otherwise become a widespread slaughter of men, both settlers and natives. After the fighting ended, the captured women and children were returned.

No direct punishment was ever meted out, but, because the settlers were anxious to get the Utes out of the country, they were relocated to Utah. Many Utes lingered in the area, however, and there was sporadic unrest, with Ute wars flaring up in 1887, and again as late as 1897.

As unfit as Meeker may have been as an agent, his stumbling endeavors in that capacity brought fame both to himself, and to the area surrounding present day Meeker.

In the fall, when aspen leaves have turned to gold, with the scrub oak bright red and the air crisp, thousands of sportsmen take to the hills in search of wild game. The hunting season turns the town of Meeker into a festival. On the first day jeeps, pickups, stationwagons and horsetrailers are on the move like some grand army marching into the high country. Teddy Roosevelt once came here searching for that prize trophy.

Along State Highway 131, twenty miles east of Meeker, is Lake Avery, boasting some of the finest fishing, boating, camping and picnicking facilities in the area. This same road from Buford follows the canyon up to Trappers Lake, situated in a great amphitheater two-thousand feet below a basalt ridge. Trapper Lake is at the base of the famous

The Bad Guys Are Gone, But The Beauty Remains

by Stan Zamonski

79

George Crouter Photograph

George Crouter Photograph

Situated in a great amphitheater 2,000 feet below a basalt ridge is Trappers Lake. Trappers Lake lies below the Flattop Wilderness, and offers excellent camping, hiking and fishing.

George Crouter Photograph

Flattop Wilderness Area. Situated on this vast plateau, ten-thousand to twelve-thousand feet above sea level, are some of the most beautiful lakes in Colorado. Deer, elk, bear, mountain sheep and lion tread this deeply shadowed forest preserve.

Forty-nine miles north of Meeker, at the crossroads of U.S. 40 and State Highway 13, is Craig. Craig is the largest city in northwest Colorado, with a populaton of about fifteen-thousand. It is the county seat of Moffat County, and offers everything from the restful solitude of the nearby mountains to the colorful atmosphere of a working cattle ranch with real cowboys. Cattle, agriculture, coal and oil come from the spreading lands of Moffat County.

This is a coldwater fishing paradise. The lofty and scenic lakes and streams hold large numbers of trophy-sized trout. In addition, fine angling for kokonee, or landlocked salmon, and whitefish is found in the area.

Situated midway along the east-west axis of the Yampa Valley, Craig has, in the last fifty years, become the largest energy and mining boomtown in the Rockies. Besides engaging in conventional strip mining, the coal companies are exploring the feasibility of leaving the deepest coal deposits underground to be burned in place. The resulting by-products would be used to replace natural gas should supplies grow scarce in the future.

Close on the heels of the miners came the gas and oil exploration firms. This mining and energy development brought a mixed bag of blessings, along with a population growth from 12,000 in 1979 to more than 15,000 in 1985.

Sixty miles to the west, on U.S. 40, is Dinosaur National Monument, a scenic and geologic wonderland easily the equal of the Grand Canyon and Yellowstone. The highway into the Monument area is a flower garden of miniature alpine flowers which you might miss if you do not take the time to stop your car and observe them at close range.

Nature had a field day when, in some pre-historic upheaval, she created the fantastic series of gorges through which rush the waters of the Green and Yampa Rivers in Dinosaur National Monument. Here, about a hundred-forty million years go, when this was a broad, marshy lowland, dinosaurs roamed and thrived in the tropical climate. From one of the fossil quarries a million pounds of pre-historic animal bones were removed. Complete skeletons of a brontosuarus and other species were excavated. Presumably these animals were mired in sand, covered with silt and buried under succeeding geological layers.

This geologic wonderland, and the float trips down the Green and Yampa rivers are great attractions to the thousands of visitors who come each year. Trained naturalists are available to answer questions about the geology of the region. From the rocky promontory of Harper's Corner, a view of Whirlpool Canyon, Steamboat Rock, Echo Park and the Canyon of Lodore spreads out before you, filled with color and majesty.

Rushing over the rapids that gash between the towering parapets in a rubber boat is one of the great adventures available to vacationers today. These activities, and the place itself, provide a

Ranching and farming, along with energy related industry, are the economic lifeblood of northwest Colorado. Scenes of ranch life abound in the picturesque valleys.

Stan Zamonski Photograph

"Woolies" have joined cattle as income producing
livestock in northwest Colorado.

wonderful opportunity for both education and inspiration.

Few places in western America have played as colorful and significant a role in forming the legends of the "Wild West" as Brown's Park. Originally known as Brown's Hole, it was named after Baptiste Brown, a French-Canadian trapper who was the first to locate in the valley.

Brown's Park is a deep mountain valley some six miles wide and forty miles long, located where the boundaries of Colorado, Utah and Wyoming come together. It is a remote no-man's land that remains almost as untamed and inaccessible today as it was in 1824, the year fur trappers first penetrated the Green River Valley, and eventually worked their way south into Brown's Park.

The isolated valley proved to be an ideal winter camp because the high mountains protected it from cold blasts, and because it was a game paradise, filled with the animals who came down from the mountains to feed. The place grew so popular with trappers that by 1837 Philip Thomson and William Craig had established a trading post. It was

primarily used as an outfitting and trading headquarters for beaver trappers, and little, if any, trading was done with the Indians.

Named Fort Davey Crockett, it was located two miles above the entrance to Lodore Canyon. The mountain men there were as wild as the game they hunted, and soon the fort became known as "the meanest in the west". The trappers were a brawling, boisterous and boozing bunch.

In 1839-40, Jim Baker and Kit Carson visited the fort while hunting in the area. Shortly after that, because of the scarcity of beaver, the trappers moved on and the fort fell into decay. A few picturesque mountain men like Baker, having found an easy life there, lingered on with their native wives until after the arrival of the first settlers.

A few settlers drifted in during the California gold rush and decided to stay, but not until the arrival of the railroad in 1868 did Brown's Park change dramatically. Major John Wesley Powell made his historic voyage through the canyon of the Green and Colorado Rivers, and it was he who officially changed the name to Brown's Park. Placer gold had

ABOVE: Piles of freshly cut hay await storage and later use as feed for the livestock of the Meeker area.

RIGHT: Probing the whitewater for trout, an angler tries his luck in the White River.

OPPOSITE: Mountain Cedar typify the stark yet strikingly beautiful flora of the arid region surrounding Dinosaur National Monument.

Stan Zamonski Photograph

**Working cattle is less romantic than one might
think. It involves a great deal of hard work, but is a
life many in northwest Colorado choose.**

been discovered in South Pass in early 1862, and it
was a flourishing gold camp even before the railroads arrived. The gold camp attracted a large
number of gamblers, bandits and horsethieves.
After the Civil War, the arrival of large herds of
cattle made Brown's Park home to cattle rustlers.

Ideal for trappers, the valley was even better as a
hideout for desparados. The many lookout points and
impregnable canyons made pursuit almost impossible. A quick ride put the outlaw across the state
line and out of a sheriff's jurisdiction. The place was
avoided by law officers.

The people who settled there adopted a live-and-
let-live attitude toward the wild characters who did
their robbing outside the park. Catching the bandits,
after all, was a job for lawmen and not for ordinary
citizens.

Among the many outlaws who moved into the
desolate canyons were Billy Bender and Les Megs,
leaders of the bloody Powder River gang. They were
followed by the celebrated bank robbers, the
McCarty brothers, who later became part of the Wild
Bunch. Brown's Park's most famous badmen were
Butch Cassidy and the Sundance Kid of the Wild

Bunch. Many stories have been written about their
sorties out of Brown's Park to rob a bank and their
dash back into "The Hole".

"Wanted, Dead or Alive" read the posters for
these men, members of the largest band of outlaws
in the history of the American West. A gang of wild
and fearless renegades, they rustled cattle, robbed,
looted and killed. Eventually the law caught up with
them. One by one they were either captured or
killed. Not one, however, was ever taken in Brown's
Park.

She might not have been the most famous, but
Ann Bassett definitely left her mark on Brown's
Park. She was known as "Queen Ann" and the title
was not an exaggeration. The "Queen's" life reads
like a Hollywood script, in fact, they must have had
her in mind when they created the TV series, "The
Big Valley", which starred Barbara Stanwick.

Ann was born a New York aristocrat, and grew to
become a woman with a petite hour glass figure. She
was as comfortable in the latest eastern fashions as
she was in buckskins. She was an excellent horse-
woman, and knew more about livestock than most
men. A crack rifle and pistol shot, she preferred

whiskey to wine, and rolled her own cigarettes. Hot-tempered, she could out cuss any man on the range. She was divorced, and made no secret of having many lovers. She was closely associated with the outlaw Wild Bunch gang (her sister Josie and Butch Cassidy had courted).

She was educated in a fine Boston finishing school, but returned to Brown's Park to work her father's ranch. Shortly after her return, she became engaged to Matt Rash, an ex-Texas Ranger. A few weeks before their wedding he was shot by Tom Horn. The west's most notorious bounty hunter, Horn was one of the very few lawmen who ever ventured into the park. Cattlemen were said to have paid him from five-hundred to eight-hundred dollars a head for cattle rustlers. They say he killed three men during his short visit; he even took a shot at "Queen Ann", but missed.

Ann was arrested and charged with rustling, but she was nobody's fool. Knowing that she was framed, she mounted a successful defense and was released. The experience may have slowed her down a little, but she never really changed. Shortly after her acquittal she married again, and remained married until her death in 1956 at the age of 78.

The story of Brown's Park doesn't end with the Wild Bunch and "Queen Ann". The legend continued with tales of lost gold mines, buried treasure and loot bandits didn't live long enough to reclaim. The final story, the "Great Diamond Fields", is one of these.

Rumors of great deposits of diamonds, rubies and emeralds by the bushel started in 1872, and soon after the rumors began, two strangers named Arnold and Slack were interviewed by the "Laramie City Sentinel". In this interview a fantastic story was told. They announced that they had discovered and worked a diamond field for two years, keeping it secret, but their operations required capital for development so they took on California investors. They were reluctant to pinpoint the location.

The Sentinel story was picked up by newspapers throughout the country, creating an excitement equal to that of the California gold rush of 1849, and that of Colorado in 1859. The entire nation was in a fever, with thousands of men eager to rush to the fields, but as yet no one knew where to go. In spite of this, thousands were already prospecting the hills of New Mexico, Arizona and Colorado.

Gradually, due largely to a series of lectures by Colorado ex-governor William Gilpin, it was believed that the San Juan Mountains near the Colorado-New Mexico line were the center of the great diamond field.

Meanwhile, Allen D. Wilson (of the U.S. Geological Survey) was riding a mule through the mountains of northern Colorado. He also had heard about the diamond discovery, but in all his explorations in the Rockies he had never seen a diamond. He and his party did, however, observe the movements of Arnold's party in the area around Brown's Park. Growing suspicious, he reported his findings

Stan Zamonski Photograph

Bow hunters pack down the results of a successful hunt. Hunting with the bow increases in popularity each year, and the abundant game of northwest Colorado attracts many sportsmen.

to Clarence King, the eminent geologist who had been hired to conduct a survey for the California investors.

King and his group set out for the diamond fields, but instead of going to Arizona or New Mexico, they travelled to Black Butte Station in Wyoming. From there they proceeded on to Colorado, eight miles from the Wyoming line. The alleged fields they discovered were in the northern part of Brown's Park. After a careful search they discovered that the widely heralded gems were indeed there, but they had been planted. The ground had been strewn with inexpensive industrial gems, some even inserted into anthills!

The investigating party returned to San Francisco and reported that some of the shrewdest capitalists in the world had been swindled by a pair of ignorant prospectors.

This was a most extravagant and interesting time in the history of the west. A time filled with countless surprises, heartbreak and adventure about which stories are still being written. This story is exceptional, but characteristic of that time and place.

Northwest Colorado is as colorful as ever. Her people as fascinating. The outlaws have moved on, but the natural beauty remains.

Dell A. McCoy Photograph

The Crystal River drains the Elk Mountains seen in the distance in this view looking south near Marble.

The Good Old Days

88

One hundred years after the miners and other settlers began to move into the upper Crystal River valley of western Colorado it is worthwhile to look back and review what the living conditions were for these intrepid pioneers. Much has been written concerning the hard work required to settle and conquer a new country, with the hardships occasioned by lack of adequate transportation, isolation and a shortage of most of the amenities we all so quickly take for granted as being essential to a civilized existence. In most of the fast-growing communities many men and even families had to live in tents for some months until log or frame houses could be built. This was the situation in Crystal City as well as in Marble during the periods of rapid growth. But primitive conditions and difficult times did not mean these people worked all the time. To enable them to survive the hard times they occasionally took time off for relaxation and enjoyment of the very special conditions and beauty which surrounded them. How did these hard-working men, women and children entertain themselves when the occasion permitted?

One person who grew up in Marble in the early 1930s remembers it this way: "It seems so long ago when I was a little girl up there and played out every day no matter what the weather was. Winter fun was a big thing and everyone had an old pair of skis, several sleds, innertubes, bob sleds and a few toboggans, and nearly everyone had some kind of ice skates. Many times we had to wait our turn to wear our brothers' or sisters' skates, and kept warm by the fire 'til our turn came around. No thought of how cold it was or how it was storming, we just made it part of our growing up and enjoyed it" (letter from Rose [Baumli] Razzano). This attitude seemed to be current among most of the children during these early days. It was a great time and a great place for them to grow up as there were plenty of things for them to do. In the summer there was the fishing, hiking and exploring in the mountains and hunting for the older boys, when their family chores were done. Winter brought its own special activities because of the snow and frozen lakes. Besides their special childish play the youngsters took part in many of their elders' recreational activities.

Social activities were very important, especially to those miners' and ranchers' families living an isolated existence. The townspeople organized many clubs and associations to foster their desire to interrelate with their fellows. The old newspapers are full of accounts of social events such as dances or "hops," parties at Halloween, St. Patrick's Day,

In Marble

by Oscar D. McCollum

Dell A. McCoy Photograph

The upper Crystal River flows past the Wild Horse Mill at Crystal City.

Participants at a 1916 party at Mrs. Carey's in Marble posed for this photograph.

Christmas, New Years' Day, or any weekend the mood struck them. The surprising thing about these "socials" was the great distance people would travel by horseback, wagon or on foot after working hard all week. In August 1887, Mrs. Dan Penny of Crystal held "a pleasant hop" and about twenty-four showed up from as far away as Prospect, Coal Basin and Thompson Creek. This is even more remarkable when one remembers that the first wagon road down the Crystal River valley was not built until five or six years later. Music for the dancing was provided by Mr. and Mrs. Wilson, vocal and instrumental music by Mrs. Andy Johnson and Miss Alice Penny as well as the Crystal River Glee Club. Supper was provided and they all danced until daylight. They then ate breakfast before starting for home.

A Halloween party at the Holland Ranch in 1909 drew 19 guests in spite of a bad storm. They were greeted with refreshments of popcorn, fresh cider and taffy which they helped "pull." Games such as pinning pasteboard hearts on a Jack O'lantern's face while blindfolded produced prizes of an imitation tomato and a hand-painted dish. Dinner was provided and "The sumptuously arrayed table showed a magician had been to work here the past half hour and had applied his magic art with a lavishing hand. Mrs. Holland was the magician." After eating they turned out the lights and gathered around the fireplace to hear ghost stories. Mr. Philips related a weird tale from Kipling. There was dancing to tunes such as "Arkansas Traveler," "Lost Indian" and other tunes of the day, played by W.W. Wood on his violin. At the end of the party the tallyho driver came to take everyone home.

Fourth of July was always an occasion for a variety of entertainments. In 1909 almost 400 persons visited Marble for the celebrations, many riding a special train with reduced fares from Glenwood Springs, New Castle and Silt. The local newspaper credited this good attendance to the special, the good roads, and an opportunity to visit the marble quarries free of charge. The celebrations started off with minor sports: races for boys and girls under 12, wheelbarrow race for men and a nail driving contest for women. Then it was time for the trip to the quarry in two specially equipped cars. In the afternoon there was a ball game between Carbondale and Marble, which the hosts lost. Next came a bucking mule contest and cow pony races followed with a 100-yard dash for men, automobile races, a picture show with a standing room only crowd extending out into the street, and after dark, fireworks were shot off from the hill above Beaver Lake. Then at 9:30 p.m., it was "On With the Dance" until 2 a.m. The day's program was planned and sponsored by the local Great Northern Scouts, and enjoyed by all.

Another form of entertainment in the valley after the turn of the century was motor car touring. The second motor car ever owned in Marble came to town in August, 1913. The machine was a 22-horsepower Metz "and it sings around these hills like a thing of life." It was owned by Dr. H.G. Haxby who was constantly with his car since its arrival and his friends twitted him abut sleeping out in the barn with it. Frank Gertig taught him how to drive and care for it and "Curb the tendency of the thing to buck and snort and climb telephone poles until now he has it pretty well tamed." The doctor was the town's first automobile bug.

The young people never were at a loss for something novel to provide a release from the tensions of the day. As in many parts of the country it was the usual custom to "serenade" newlyweds by their peers. In July, 1923 this opportunity presented itself when "three gallant young men, John Parsons, Tom

Members of the Marble Church Sunday School pose in their Sunday best.

Marble May Day parade passes in front of the Parry and Wood homes.

Kissel and W.J. Hodgson, each with a June bride'' returned to town. The three young couples were so engrossed in their own raptures they naively assumed they had escaped the custom. By ''clever tactics'' the three couples were captured and placed in the People's Store under guard while an express wagon was confiscated. ''The benedicts and the brides were forced into the conveyance and drawn by a happy, noisy crowd to the camping grounds where Strickland's orchestra was camping, and given their choice to negotiate for a free dance or go to jail.'' After initial objections the newlywoods quickly arranged for the music, spurred on by the town marshal's presumed backing of the threat, and all repaired to the Masonic Hall and danced until eleven o'clock to everyone's enjoyment. The occasion offered a favorable time for a general introduction to the brides while the husbands were tied in a corner as the crowd danced with their wives.

Dancing was probably one of the most popular forms of entertainment and was sponsored by various groups, or occurred spontaneously. The local volunteer firemen were often the instigators, with the help of the Marble Band, either for free or as a money-raiser. In 1921 the townspeople held a party and dance to celebrate the opening of the quarry and mill after the wartime closing. A notice in the *Crystal River Current* as early as 1886 informed the boys of the Crystal River to ''Look out for the grand ball and supper at the Elk Mountain House on New Year's Eve at Crested Butte.'' Indications are that a number of the husky bachelors crossed the forbidding Schofield Pass through the deep snow to enjoy an evening. The twenty mile trip was undertaken as casually as if they were reporting to a local silver mine for work. Those who did not wish to go to that lively town were cordially invited to a New Year's dinner in Crystal given by Mrs. G.W. Melton.

The Marble Hall on State Street in Marble was available in 1910 for Hops, Entertainments, Social Gatherings, and Gabfests. In 1916 there was a social dance at the Crystal Club in Crystal, which ''now has a piano.'' The O.N.O. Dancing Club offered a turkey supper and dance in 1912 for 109 members and guests. The Walsh family catered, and the dances included: waltzes, two steps, schottisches, with ''Chains'' and ''Tags.'' Dancing and entertainment were offered by the Emanon Club at its party in March 1913, and the next year there was a Nickel Dance at the Masonic Hall on July fourth. Music for the dances often was provided by Paul Tischhouser and his orchestra of six pieces: Piano, violin, clarinet, cornet, trombone and drums. Fourth of July dances had the entire Marble Band in attendance. Leo Liston sometimes played the piano, sometimes with drums and coronet joining in.

Miscellaneous entertainments included the 1912 firemen's ''smokeless'' smoker at the pool hall with amateur boxing, an Italo-Greek picnic the same year, trips to Redstone (by special train for 50 cents) for dancing, horseshoe pitching, marble pitching by children, and many picnics in Lead King Basin and other popular spots. Oldtimers swapped yarns whenever they got together.

Winter sports occupied a top position from the beginning in this beautiful area of pristine powder snow. By December of each year the wagon road over Schofield Pass was closed by snow and the mail had to be carried from Crested Butte to Crystal on the backs of men traveling on skis. These skis, which in the 1880s were called snow shoes, were made by hand from boards nine feet long. Those used by Ambrose Williams are in the Aspen museum. They were needed in winter to reach many of the

This photograph taken circa 1910, captures the May Day festivities at the Marble band stand.

Discarded blocks of marble lay beside the abandoned Crystal River & San Juan Railroad grade at Marble.

operating mines and the men became quite daring and skillful. By 1886 the Gunnison County Snowshoe Club had been organized and consisted of members from all over the county. A small group of members from Crystal and Schofield, including Tom Boughton, Frank Williams, Al and Fred Johnson, usually ran off with the prizes and became quite cocky. They would issue challenges to all comers and prizes might be as much as $150, $75 and $25 for first, second and third places (substantial amounts in those days). Club winners often entered state championships. Frank Williams' skis were called the Devil's shoes. On one occasion the Crystal River members challenged Ouray and Silverton skiers to race any of the following ways: "Fastest speed downhill, with or without pole, or take another man, weight not less than 135 pounds, on their shoulders and run down, or they will run on level ground with or without a pack, from 500 yards to 50 miles, if to travel with pack take anywhere from 25 to 100 pounds. Alternatives: run downhill on one shoe, run down with two men standing on one pair shoes, or two men on three shoes, or three men on four shoes, or run down with rider facing up hill" (*The Marble Booster*, 1887). A.A. Johnson, who ran a store in Crystal, sometimes carried the mail from Crested Butte to Crystal over Schofield Pass and down the Crystal River gorge past the Devil's Punch Bowl. Once, someone asked how he had the nerve to ski down the canyon with its avalanche danger. He replied that he pushed off hard at the top and went as fast as possible in hopes of outrunning any avalanches. This technique always worked for him. Much enthusiasm was whipped up over the "snow shoe" races held by the Gunnison County Club at Crested Butte, Gothic and Gunnison. Many men were not occupied during much of the winter and were willing to spend several days traveling to these contests. The *Current* reported on a race at Crested Butte in 1887 with headlines: "Our Winter's Sport, Crested Butte Opens up the SnowShow Season With a Grand Race." The race scheduled for a Sunday was postponed until Monday on account of a snow storm. "A large crowd came out on snow-shoes and in sleighs to witness the fun, among them were all the young ladies who highly enjoyed the tramp on shoes. A splendid track was selected, north of town, on what is known as the Chicken Ranch hill, and a course laid out to run three at a time. Ten entries were made and the winner of two heats laid off for the final run to determine the winner of the prizes..." Frank Williams and Tom Boughton were the 1st and 2nd prize winners. "After the race several young ladies climbed the hill to make the descent, showing splendid skill in the art of snow-shoeing." The club painted the town red. "Capt. Burton eat [sic] too much dinner to be present at the race." The club challenged any shoers in the United States or Canada. Their view of the sport is clearly revealed by the following poem:

Our Winter Sport
(written for the Current by D. Evil)

"'Tis not a sport of childhood,
    Nor is it called a play;
It always does our old folks good,
    And makes the young folks gay.

It gives our lassies bright red cheeks,
    And our laddies those of brown;
It makes the old folks pleasure seek,
    And of all sports it's the crown.

For you always get plenty exercise
    While climbing up the hill;
And when descending how the snow flies
    When you show your acrobatic skill.

It is the sport of sports of all sports,
    This one we cherish so—
It is justly called the open port
    Of Heaven here below.

In wonder, no longer will I keep you,
    But straight-way let you know,
That it is the Norweigan snow-shoe
    We use for gliding o'er the snow.

Now just try this little episode,
    Then straight-way let me know;
How many successive times you dove
    Head-first in the snow."

Perhaps all the skiers were not expert as a later story reports: "A course has been cleared through the timber on Mineral Point above Crystal for snow-shoeing and the boys have great sport tumbling."
Bobsledding was a popular sport. A course was

Marble Historical Society Collection

This early day fish catch near Marble demonstrates the abundance of trout then present.

93

Band music was an important form of entertainment in early day Marble.

made on Main Street from the Marble high school building down through the center of town all the way to Beaver Lake. The fire department sprinkled the street with water to form ice and some merchants estimated that the bobsleds raced past their establishments at speeds up to 55 miles per hour. They raced even at night and there were a number of accidents when someone failed to get out of the way in time or when the sleds turned over in the snow. At one point a town councilman promised to install a street light at West Second to make the course safer.

One of the popular sports was fishing in the river and lakes for trout. Game limits were high or ignored and newspaper reports indicated catches of 30 and 40 fish. The Marble museum displays a net fish trap used at Crystal before 1900. The large catches depleted the fish in the river and efforts were made to get the county to build a fish hatchery. By 1913 the Sportsmens' Club was working to improve fishing. Many easterners were so impressed with the fishing in the Crystal River they came all the way out here to spend their vacations.

All kinds of sports were enjoyed. The town had a baseball team, complete with uniforms, and played teams from nearby towns. Teams came to Marble from New Castle and Carbondale, and in August 1913, the Marble team won a game against the Spring Gulch boys, 10 to 4. The Marble ball field had a grandstand holding 200 people. In 1910 the Marble Association Foot-Ball Club bragged that its coach was Bob Williams, a native of Wales who had coached at Johns Hopkins University last season (he was now a marble worker). It also had several good players from Scotland, England and Ireland.

Moving picture theaters were popular and had shows Friday and Sunday evenings, and in 1916 Joe Faussone's Marble Theatre advertized that a four piece orchestra played at each performance, and prices were 25 cents for adults and 15 cents for children. Four years earlier, he had proudly called his establishment the Marble Opera House, though no evidence can be found of any opera performances.

Fraternal organizations were plentiful, with the Masonic Lodge No. 137 being organized in 1910. It owned its own two-story building with a popular dance floor upstairs. In the same year the Brotherhood of American Yeomen, Homestead No. 2233, and the Fraternal Order of Eagles, Marble Aerie No. 1827, were organized. Both met twice monthly. Two years later the Homesteaders' Lodge was organized and the Marble Hive No. 9, L.O.T.M. was in existence. The Woodsmen of the World, Camp No. 702 was active through many years and in 1913 ordered fifty monuments of marble to be placed around the country, as well as several "Temples of Fame" chapels. A tombstone it placed can still be seen in the Marble cemetery. The Elks were also in evidence and held a convention in Marble in the 1920s.

The churches in Marble were an important social element. In 1908, Col. Meek, president of the Yule-Colorado Marble Co., donated two lots, and the St. John's Episcopal church building in Aspen was dismantled and moved to the Marble site and renamed St. Paul's. Church services of several denominations were held in this building. For a few years an

Lodges and fraternal organizations were popular throughout Colorado in the early days. These are the charter members of the A.F.A.M., Marble Lodge Number 137.

Episcopal priest was assigned to Marble but after World War I priests usually came for services from Aspen or Glenwood Springs. The Women's Auxiliary, the Ladies' Aid Society of the Union Church and the Lady Maccabees supported the work of the churches with luncheons, bazaars, teas and bobsled rides.

Other clubs included the Ladies' Auction Club, a Boys Club organized by the Rev. Oliver Kingman, which met in the library building behind the church. This library was stocked with books and periodicals donated by the stockholders of the marble company and members of the church congregation. The high school Literary Club encouraged reading among the youth. The Frost lending library offered memberships at 75 cents with book rentals at 10 cents per week, and had 600 first class fiction volumes.

A sewing club called the Columbine Club met regularly and one summer its girls presented a ladies black-face minstrel show at the Faussone Theater, with music by the high school orchestra. In 1927, The Marble Sportsmen Club was organized and sponsored Troop No. 128, Boy Scouts of America, which functioned for several years.

As in most mining towns, Marble boasted several saloons where the men could relax from their labors with a drink and convivial conversation. Among the early saloons were counted the Silver Dollar Saloon, the Taaley & Heberling Saloon and Joe Faussone's Senate Saloon. At the urging of the marble company the town citizens voted in 1909 to become dry and all saloons disappeared. The large number of Italian and eastern European marble workers liked their liquor, so secret stills and bootlegging became a big industry which could not be controlled by the many ordinances passed by the town council.

This thirst and the need for places to gather was partially met by the New Pastime Parlor, offering soft drinks and cigars, under Joe Gallo's management. Winn & Brownell opened the Mission Billiard Parlor which also sold cigars and tobacco, candies and gum.

Marble and Crystal probably were not much different from many other isolated mining towns: the residents were left to their own devices in providing opportunities for recreation and relaxation from their labors. Their attempts to provide entertainment were varied and in the high and beautiful mountains of the upper Crystal River valley they took advantage of what nature provided. Modern recreational developments have grown from the base provided by their predecessors.

Cripple Creek's Fortune In Gold

by Jeremy Agnew

The road that goes to Cripple Creek leads west from Colorado Springs on U.S. Highway 24, up Ute Pass, to Divide. From there paved Colorado state highway 67 starts south and rapidly winds its way up through the pine and aspen trees, its steepness increasing. Then, at 9,500 feet, the road passes over the final crest and there lies Cripple Creek at the bottom of a bowl-shaped valley that is the heart of an ancient extinct volcano.

The barren rock-strewn hills unfolding before you look as if an army of giant gophers had ravaged the land, digging holes then heaping up little piles of rubble everywhere. Mine hoists, their timbers blackened by time and the elements, stand with boards sagging and collapsing to the ground. It is hard to imagine that these empty windswept hills were once alive with thousands of miners, who had flocked from all over the world to dig for their fortunes in one of the greatest gold camps that the world has ever known.

Gold! That was the magic word responsible for Cripple Creek and for much of the settling and development of early Colorado. This precious yellow metal has nourished man's dreams and fed his hopes from the early days of history. Its discovery in the mountains of Colorado brought a steady stream of hopefuls out west to seek their fortunes. Some of them achieved this goal. Most did not. But before the gold rush era was over, the Cripple Creek area was to become the second largest gold-producing district in the world, pouring out a total of over $430,000,000 worth of gold. During the year 1900 alone, there were 475 operating mines in the district that produced over $18,000,000 worth of gold.

But in spite of all this, Cripple Creek's beginnings were humble enough. In the 1870s and 1880s when Colorado mining camps like Central City, Leadville, Creede and Aspen were booming both figuratively and literally with the explosions of miners' dynamite, the high mountain meadow that would become Cripple Creek was slumbering quietly on the other side of Pikes Peak from Colorado Springs.

The discovery of the Cripple Creek bonanza that would rock the gold mining world was delayed by several factors. One of the main ones was that Cripple Creek gold did not look like the gold traditionally mined at that time. Early gold mining in Colorado was for free gold, actual flakes, and sometimes nuggets, of pure metal that had the gleaming yellow luster that we all associate with the word gold. Cripple Creek's riches, on the other hand, were in the form of complex ores of gold and silver tellurides that look most uninteresting and which require complex processing to extract the pure gold metal. Instead of occurring in streambeds and quartz outcroppings as were being mined in the rest of the state, Cripple Creek's gold ore was deposited in narrow cracks and fissures in the hard granite underlying the rolling green meadows. The few early hopefuls who prospected around Cripple Creek found only some dirty-looking grey and yellow rocks, so they moved on to other richer strikes.

Only one man persevered.

It took 12 years for Bob Womack to find the bonanza that he was convinced was around Cripple Creek somewhere. He even became known as "Crazy Bob" for continuing to prospect after the "experts" had decided that there was no gold present. But Bob persevered and poked around the hills behind Pikes Peak until 1890, the year in which he staked out a claim on a vein that assayed out at several hundred dollars per ton—a veritable bonanza. After the gold rush started, Bob Womack stepped back into obscurity. Sadly he was not to profit from the millions of dollars worth of gold that he had shown to the world. He eventually sold his El Paso claim for $500 and died almost penniless in Colorado Springs in 1909.

Because of the random nature of the ore veins under the ground, Cripple Creek miners could only sink shafts at random through the solid rock and hope that they would hit a rich ore vein. Some early miners miscalculated and dug shafts only feet away from major discoveries, and then stopped in discouragement without knowing that they were close to huge fortunes. To illustrate this, there is the story of the two druggists from Colorado Springs who staked out the Pharmacist mine. Unconvinced of scientific mining methods, they threw a hat into the air and then dug where it landed. They were lucky and hit rich ore.

The town of Cripple Creek itself was started in 1891 by Horace Bennett and Julius Myers, two

Jeremy Agnew Photograph

The huge Gold Coin mine works were built in downtown Victor after rich ore was found during excavation for a hotel.

Denver real estate brokers who bought Bob Womack's original homestead as an investment. When the gold-seekers started pouring into the area, Bennett and Myers shelved any plans for ranching and platted the land for a townsite. There are various tall tales surrounding the naming of the town as Cripple Creek; the most consistent ones relate that the town was named for the many accidents that happened to people and livestock along the banks of the little stream that crossed the valley.

The main east-west street was named Bennett Avenue and the next street to the south was named Myers Avenue. Bennett Avenue was to become the town's business district, lined with banks, saloons, mining supply houses and hardware stores. Little did Julius Myers know that his Myers Avenue was later to become one of the best-known red light districts in the state, complete with saloons, dance halls, parlor houses, gambling halls and one-girl cribs.

Statistics on the early growth of Cripple Creek are vague and probably colored by optimistic town promoters, but it appears that in 1890 (the year before the founding of the town) the population of the area was 15. By 1896 there were about 15,000 people scattered around the hills—not a bad start for a five year old town. The early miners' conception of priorities is clear: in 1896 there were six churches and two banks, but there were 73 saloons. Today the present population of Cripple Creek is back down to about 650 people.

Cripple Creek was not the only town in the area. Wherever gold was found, people followed. Settlements sprang up all over the place and had exotic names such as Arequa, Mound City, Altman, Elkton, Grassy, Midway, Goldfield and Independence.

The area's population reached a peak in 1901, then started into a period of gradual but increasing decline from which it never recovered. One of the major factors in the decline was increasing labor relations problems.

Labor problems started in 1893 with a dispute between the mine owners and the miners over the length of the work shift and the pay scales. The result was a four month strike that included skirmishes between union and non-union workers, and a pitched battle between the miners and the militia, which was sent in to help keep peace. Over the following decades further labor problems, water in the lower mine levels, two World Wars, changing prices of gold, the closing of the railroads, rising production costs and falling profits forced many of the mines to close, never to reopen.

But while mining creaked to a standstill in the 1950s, another industry was having its quiet beginnings in Colorado. Tourism, which had been on the increase in the Rockies for a number of years, found an ideal ally in Cripple Creek.

Cripple Creek has built up many scenic attractions over the years. In 1946, Wayne and Dorothy Mackin

bought and subsequently restored the Imperial Hotel on Third Street. Every summer they present a series of melodramas in the Gold Bar Room Theater. At a typical performance, visitors from all over the United States are gathered to cheer the hero and boo the villain as his dastardly plots are thwarted.

The old Midland Terminal railroad depot at the east end of Bennett Avenue was converted in 1953 into a museum filled with memorabilia of the early mining days. The Mollie Kathleen and El Paso mines have shown thousands of interested visitors the inner workings of real gold mines. Since 1967 the Cripple Creek and Victor Narrow Gauge Railroad has carried children (of all ages) in its brightly colored tiny open coaches pulled by miniature steam engines. The toll road up the 10,400 foot high cone of Mount Pisgah has impressed visitors with its 360° panoramic view of Pikes Peak, the Sangre de Cristo mountains and the snowcapped peaks of the

Short Line train crosses Devil's Slide on the way to Cripple Creek. A horse drawn wagon can be seen on the stage road below.

ABOVE: A view of Bennett Avenue, Cripple Creek, looking east past the courthouse (on the left) to the museum at the end of the street.

The abandoned ruins of the old saloon at Midway, above Cripple Creek.

Cathedral Park along the Gold Camp Road.

Jeremy Agnew Photograph

Jeremy Agnew Photograph

The huge hoist frame of the Portland Mine on Battle Mountain near Victor.

The town of Victor, with the Strong Mine on the right and the Florence and Cripple Creek railroad yards in the center, is the subject of this photograph.

Continental Divide. For those who also want to see how the other half lived, the Old Homestead Parlor House, a restored Victorian pleasure house in the Myers Avenue red light district can be visited with complete respectability.

Though there are several roads in and out of Cripple Creek, the most interesting way to reach the town today is via the 45 mile long Gold Camp Road from Colorado Springs. This popular scenic highway is built on the old road bed of the Colorado Springs and Cripple Creek District Railway, more popularly known as the Short Line. The present road still goes through several of the old railroad tunnels.

Even in its heyday as a railroad, the Short Line was well known as a scenic ride and was very popular for day excursions. Vice-president Theodore Roosevelt made the trip to Cripple Creek in 1901 and is reported to have said, "This is the trip that bankrupts the English language." The railroad carried freight and passengers for many years before its closing in 1920, then in 1924 the railbed was reopened as a scenic toll auto highway. Today it is a free, state-owned road.

As the modern roadway winds up to Cripple

Creek, it provides some sweeping views of the plains. In the fall, when the aspen trees start to turn to gold, even the local residents load up their picnic baskets and enjoy Nature's show of color on the route that carried much of Cripple Creek's gold to the mills near Colorado Springs.

Though Cripple Creek received all the credit, the town of Victor five miles away to the southeast was the town with most of the mines. Victor's nickname was the "City of Mines". Battle Mountain, just to the north of Victor, was the richest gold-producing area in the district, and shipped far more gold than did Cripple Creek proper. The town of Cripple Creek was the center of the mining district's social, commercial and financial activities, while Victor was somewhat looked down on as a working town where the miners lived in order to be close to their work.

The large Gold Coin mine was discovered by accident in downtown Victor while excavation was underway for a new hotel. The ore discovered was so rich that plans for the new hotel were quickly forgotten and the Gold Coin mine was dug instead. As the mine was in the middle of downtown Victor there was nowhere to dump the waste rock, so the in-

Fires were common in early mining towns, and
Victor was no exception.

genious solution was to dig a tunnel 7/10 of a mile
through Squaw Mountain into Arequa Gulch to the
east. At the other end of the tunnel the owners
erected a mill and processed the ore right as it came
from the ore cars. The brick foundations of the
Economic Gold Extraction Company mill can still be
seen on the steep hillside of Arequa Gulch between
Cripple Creek and Victor. The practice of building a
processing mill on a hillside like this was typical as it
allowed the ore to flow by gravity through the
various stages of processing.

Finally, no account of Cripple Creek would be
complete without mentioning Gillett and the story of
the only bullfight held in the United States. The
abandoned town of Gillett lies about four miles
northeast of Cripple Creek, along the side of State
Highway 67 from Divide. The town was started in
1894 along the tracks of the Midland Terminal railroad, which ran until 1949. Gillett's real reason for
being though, was a racetrack erected by two Cripple
Creek mine owners who enjoyed horse racing.

In August of 1895, two promoters, named Arizona
Charlie Meadows and Joe Wolfe, rented the racetrack to stage a real live Mexican bullfight. All the
arrangements were made, professional bullfighters
were engaged, tickets were sold and the great day
arrived. Unfortunately for Wolfe, the Humane
Society of Colorado Springs viewed the upcoming
spectacle with distaste and arranged to stop im-
portation of the bulls from Mexico. The enterprising
Wolfe scrounged up some local stock to take their
place, and the show proceeded. After two rather
mediocre performances, the El Paso county sheriff
arrested the whole lot of them and cancelled all
further performances.

Gillett has pretty much returned to grazing land,
but the foundation of the old race track can still be
seen as an oval depression in the ground, just to the
east of the highway. That and a few old buildings
that are left are all that remain to remind passers-by
of the only bullfight to take place in the United
States.

Jeremy Agnew Photograph

ABOVE: Cripple Creek sits in a bowl-shaped valley at the bottom of an extinct volcano.

The restored Imperial Hotel presents Victorian melodramas in Cripple Creek each summer in its Gold Barroom Theater.

Jeremy Agnew Photograph

Cripple Creek and Victor Narrow Gauge Railroad locomotive Number 1 rests at the depot museum in Cripple Creek. This two-foot gauge Mallet still runs toward Victor.

I stopped suddenly and blinked. Straight ahead of me, on the top of the sand dune, was a huge palomino horse. He was standing with all four legs planted defiantly in the sand; his head was upraised in mute challenge, and his mane and tail streamed like pennants in the wind. Then he turned and, apparently not seeing me, started galloping down the side of the dune, his large webbed feet splaying out and hardly seeming to touch the sand.

I rubbed my eyes and blinked again. When I looked back at the top of the dune, there was nothing there. I could hear only the quiet whispering of the wind as it carried tiny grains of sand up the face of the dune, only to push them over the crest and down the other side.

I had fallen prey to the legends of the Sand Dunes and had imagined one of the very stories I had heard from one of the old-timers.

There was no sign of tracks marring the smooth, creamy expanse of the sand dune. The golden sand seemed to smile at me in satisfaction. I smiled back and struggled on up to the crest of the dune.

One of the most unusual natural phenomena in Colorado is the Great Sand Dunes. Nestled up against the Sangre de Cristo mountains, on the east side of the San Luis Valley, are huge dunes of sand rising more than 700 feet into the air. Formally named the Great Sand Dunes National Monument, these incalculable tons of sand are spread over an area of 50 square miles, like a miniature Sahara desert. Shunned by early explorers and settlers for their lack of water and fertile soil for crops, the Sand Dunes today are a popular attraction for visitors and Colorado residents alike.

I paused to catch my breath and reflect on this as I toiled my way up the side of one of the dunes. It was only May; but, already, in the late morning, the temperature felt like it was in the high eighties and the sun's heat reflected back by the light yellow sand was scorching. It was hard work climbing up the sand. On every step up my boots sank into the sand, and the tiny grains, like thousands of ball-bearings, immediately started to shift downhill under my weight.

I looked back down. The night-time breeze had erased all the tracks in the sand from the day before and now only my footprints could be seen zigzagging their path up the smooth white face of the dune. The dry sand shifted so easily that my footprints were already blurred and partially filled in.

Way down below, at the end of my zigzagging trail of prints, I could see the broad, flat expanse of Medano Creek, surging in ripples as it flowed down across the sand from high up in the Sangre de Cristo mountains. As it was early in the year, the creek was still running, fed by snowmelt water; although it was only an inch or two deep in most places. In a couple of months the creek would be gone - swallowed up by the searing heat of the white sand and the soaring daytime temperatures. But for now it was still there, glinting in the morning sun as the ripples flowed smoothly across the flat sand.

On the far side of the creek I could see my wife and daughter, looking like tiny ants way down below me. My wife was sitting on the bank enjoying the warm sun and watching our little girl running and splashing in the shallow water with the joy of youth.

Further behind them, at the edge of the trees, I could see the orange and blue of nylon tents and the gleaming of the sun on the car windows and chrome bumpers that outlined the Park Service campground. A couple of trails of blue smoke drifted lazily up from among the campsites, where someone was already cooking lunch over a fire-grate.

The pounding in my chest, due to the vigorous climb I had been making, had slowed down so I turned uphill and started climbing again. When I reached the crest of the dune, I sat down and surveyed the view that had unfolded before me. Heading to the north was a seemingly endless sea of sand with crests and waves rolling like an ocean frozen in time. Though I couldn't see their northern boundary, I knew it was about 10 miles away.

Colorado's Mysterious Sand Dunes

by Jeremy Agnew

107

ABOVE: A sea of sand rises from the floor of the San Luis Valley in this aerial photograph.

Waves of sand lap against the Sangre de Cristo Mountains.

OPPOSITE: The snow-capped peaks of the Sangre de Cristo rise above the dunes.

In the distance, rising up behind the dunes were the jaggedly upthrust peaks of the Sangre de Cristo mountains. I could recognize Crestone Peak and Crestone Needle with their snow-capped peaks making a beautiful contrast against the deep blue of the Colorado morning sky.

At my feet I watched the gently blowing breeze bounce grains of sand up the side of the dune and over the top, to let them dance gaily down the other side until they finally came to rest. There was only the soft sighing sound of the wind constantly re-shaping the dunes. I felt at peace with the world.

These sand dunes I was sitting on were built up a grain at a time by the wind that blows almost cease-lessly out of the southwest, across the floor of the San Luis valley. Most of the sand is composed of tiny particles of volcanic rock that came originally from the San Juan mountains, about 50 miles to the west across the valley. These grains of sand were broken from the mountains by weathering over the ages, and were carried down by the infant Rio Grande River, which has its headwaters in the San Juans, to form the sandy soil of the San Luis Valley floor. The Rio Grande has changed its course several times in the past, and as it meandered about the valley floor it left tons of gravel and sand in oxbows and levees, and in its old riverbeds.

From the valley floor, the sand has been blown by the prevailing southwesterly winds to the base of the mountains. The sand travels generally along the ground, rising into the air a few inches at a time in a sort of hopping motion called saltation. The Sangre de Cristo mountains, which form a natural barrier to the wind, have a low spot bounded by 14,338 foot Blanca Peak and 14,037 foot Little Bear Peak on the south, and 14,294 foot Crestone Peak and 14,191 foot Crestone Needle on the north.

This natural pocket forms the path of least resistance for the wind; so, laden with sand, it rushes up the sides of the pocket and bursts through three relatively low passes - Mosca Pass (9,713 feet); Medano Pass (9,900 feet); and Music Pass (11,800 feet) - at the top of the mountains. The sand grains are too heavy to be carried up and over the moun-tains, so the wind drops them right at the base of the mountains where, over geologic eons, they have accumulated to form the Sand Dunes.

Under normal conditions with the eastward pre-vailing winds, at least part of the dunes would shift slowly to the east into the mountains; however, strong storm winds periodically blasting back down out of the Sangre de Cristos have tended to counter-act this and keep the dunes in a relatively stable location. These two winds - the gentle winds from the west and the strong storms from the east - are responsible for the general shape of the dunes, which typically have long gentle slopes up from the west and more abrupt slopes on the east, often with reversing crests at the top.

Photographs taken 50 years ago show the dunes much as they appear now. Even though they are on the move constantly, they tend to stay in the same general location, endlessly shaped and reshaped by the wind.

The constant movement of the sand, the less than eight inches of rainfall that the San Luis valley receives over a year, and the more than 140°F summertime surface temperature of the sand make it difficult for any vegetation to grow in the dunes themselves. A few scurfpeas, with tiny purplish-blue blossoms; some sunflowers, topped by their colorful yellow blooms; spiky-looking blowout-grass; and the Indian ricegrass, with its cloud of seedheads, form the only vegetation growing in some of the protected hollows among the dunes.

Because of the dryness, the lack of water and the scarcity of food, very few animals venture into the dunes themselves, though an occasional coyote may be seen prowling the edges of the dunes looking for a meal. One of the tidbits that the coyote is looking for is the kangaroo rat, a tiny desert-loving rodent whose body is so highly attuned to its environment that it does not have to drink water. It does not sweat and its internal system is so efficient that it has minimized water losses from excretion; also, it can actually manufacture enough water to exist inside its own body, a byproduct of the seeds it eats.

As you move out beyond the edge of the dunes and into the ponderosa pine forest, vegetation and animals become more prominent. Prickly pear cactus, ring muhly, grama grass, wild four-o'clocks and blazing stars put in their appearance. Deer, rabbits, coyotes and chipmunks can be found. Birds, such as Steller's jay, the black-billed magpie and the broad-tailed hummingbird are also seen on the fringes of the dunes. If you are lucky you may even see a golden eagle soaring overhead, looking for a meal.

The Sand Dunes are easily accessible from two directions. From the west, State 150 comes in frm the highway between Poncha Springs and Alamosa. To the south, there is a road that comes up from U.S. Highway 160 between La Veta Pass and Alamosa.

For the more adventurous there is a rough four-wheel-drive-only road that comes in from the east side, from Gardner, over the Sangre de Cristo mountains at 9,900 foot Medano Pass (Medano is Spanish for sand dune), and follows alongside Medano Creek off the top of the pass. The bottom part of the road is actually through Medano Creek, made treacherous in the spring by quicksand and running water.

There are two other passes through the mountains from the dunes. To the south of the Sand Dunes is Mosca Pass which used to be an old wagon road for settlers and supply trains when the San Luis Valley was being colonized. The name Mosca means "fly" in Spanish, and was given to the pass by the early Spanish explorers who passed through the area. The pass was used for many years by sheepherders taking their sheep to summer pasture. Today, the former rough, rocky wagon road is an interesting

Steven J. Meyers Photograph

trail that winds 3½ miles from just east of the visitor center to the top of the pass. The other pass, Music Pass, is to the north of the dunes. The name Music comes from the weird sighing and moaning noises of the wind whistling through the pass. Music Pass crosses the Sangre de Cristos south of Crestone Needle, then follows Sand Creek down to the north edge of the dunes, near the few remaining dilapidated buildings of the old ghost town of Liberty.

Early explorers and settlers to the San Luis Valley found that the three passes were natural passages in the mountains and used them to gain access to the valley. The earliest recorded reference to the Sand Dunes is in the journal of Zebulon Pike, whose name is remembered for Pikes Peak; later Captain John Fremont and Captain John Gunnison recrossed the area on their exploratory expeditions.

Along with the legends of the ghost horses with their webbed feet flying across the dunes in the moonlight, there are many legends of people and the

The effects of wind are seen in the ripples which cover much of the surface of the dunes.

OVERLEAF: Medano Creek, with its wide variation of seasonal flow, rushes past the cottonwoods at the south edge of the dunes.

Jeremy Agnew Collection

111

dunes. One of the most often retold is about the wagon train that came over Mosca Pass late one day and stopped for the night alongside the dunes by Medano Creek, where the wagons were drawn up and the mules unhitched. After a welcome rest and evening meal, the drivers bedded down for the night. The next morning the mules and wagons had mysteriously disappeared without a trace. Where did they go? No one knows for sure. The most likely explanation is that they vanished into the quicksand in the creek.

And there are the stories of the settlers and their wagons, and the Mexican sheepherders and their flocks, all of whom disappeared without a trace. Nobody knows for sure about any of them either. What is certain is that the Sand Dunes hold many secrets. Occasionally the shifting winds will uncover an old wagon wheel, or some horseshoes, or some personal belongings of the settlers who travelled past. One can only wonder what other stories lie hidden in the sand.

Medano Creek with its spring waters and quicksand is probably responsible for some of the mysterious disappearances of the legends. Medano Creek is a strictly seasonal river - if it can even be called a river. It flows down out of the Sangre de Cristo mountains when the warm days of spring start to melt the snow high on the mountain peaks. By early summer it is a sheet of water flowing across the sand and forming the south boundary of the dunes proper. It is very wide - over a hundred feet in places - but it is only a few inches deep in most places and makes an ideal place for children (and us grown-up children) to enjoy a little of the ocean-and-beach atmosphere. At the end of the dunes, the river eventually sinks into the sand.

As summer progresses, the creek dwindles, flowing only for part of the day, then it finally disappears into the sand completely for the rest of the year.

In years past, Indians, early Spanish explorers, farmers, sheepmen, cattle ranchers, and even hopeful gold miners have crisscrossed the area, but none penetrated the dunes themselves. The dry, barren sand, constantly shifting and moving, was no good for any of the everyday activities of life, such as farming or homesteading, so the dunes were left untouched.

However, in 1932, President Hoover proclaimed the area a National Monument and, ever since then, steadily increasing streams of visitors have come to marvel, admire, explore and enjoy the mysterious shifting mountains of sand that are Colorado's Sand Dunes.

OPPOSITE: Trapped in an eddy created by the mountain barrier, sand grains collected to form the great dunes.

Steven J. Meyers Photograph

Dell A. McCoy Photograph

Locomotive Number 481 is bucking snow at the
Silverton Depot in November of 1982. Thanks to an
extended operating schedule on the Durango and
Silverton Narrow Gauge Railroad, riders are now
able to witness scenes such as these, and view the
San Juans with their winter mantel of snow.

The Durango & Silverton Narrow Gauge Railroad

by William R. Jones

The young hiker looked at his watch and stepped up his pace. His feet pounded, and his back ached from a week in the Weminuche Wilderness. Still, he forced himself to take bigger steps on the narrow trail along Elk Creek. A rock rabbit chirped at him, as if to say, "What's your hurry?"

"I have a train to catch," the hiker replied, "the Silverton Train."

Soon the rushing Animas River was in view. River of Lost Souls is what the Spanish called it, but to the hiker and the prospectors before him it showed the way to civilization. Barely visible along the river bank was the narrow-gauge track of the Durango and Silverton Railroad. Though spiked down of heavy steel rails over one hundred years ago, it seemed like a mere child's toy amid the towering rock spires of Mount Garfield.

Finally the hiker reached the deserted siding. A couple of old wooden boxcars sat amid dry weeds and the pungent pile of creosote ties. "Elk Park", the faded sign said. It looked real enough now, yet everything he had seen in the past week had a sur-realistic quality. The mountains were oversized and young, the railroad seemed half scale and old. The crooked line of cars looked like grandpa's faded pictures, made color, made real again.

Suddenly, above the constant rush of the river, came the clear tones of a whistle! A yellowish patch of smoke came floating up through the quaking aspen leaves, their brilliant gold color glowing in the autumn sun. Then the staccato chuffing could be heard, like someone running hard but refusing to slow down. The black locomotive rounded the bend and bore down on the hiker. Its yellow headlight glowed like a cyclops eye on this snorting beast doing a jerky dance down the track. The hiker took off his red bandana and stepped hesitantly onto the track.

"You have to stand facing the engine and wave a flag across the tracks," they told him in Durango, "don't just wave hello. The engineer will think you're friendly but won't stop."

Like a bullfighter facing the charge, he waved the red flag. To his relief, the engineer gave an acknowl-

Richard A. Bell Photograph

Charles Bradshaw (on left) prepares to cut the ribbon celebrating the beginning of operations of his new railroad on May 5, 1981.

Richard A. Bell Photograph

Locomotives Number 473 and Number 476 simmer in the Durango yard. The Durango depot can be seen on the left.

edging toot and backed off the throttle. Amid the steaming hiss and squeal of brakes, the conductor, dressed incongruously in gold braid, hat, tie, but ordinary overalls, leaned out and motioned him aboard. After paying a cash fare, the tired hiker took a seat in an old oak paneled coach. The train whistled off, and with a gentle tug they were moving again.

The ride was a relief after the ordeal of the high mountain wilderness. The old coach was a real rolling antique, with brass doorknobs, wooden luggage racks and a pot belly stove in the corner. The wood panels squeaked in protest as the car twisted around the tight curves, only inches from the boiling river water, or so it seemed. The sweet odor of coal smoke drifted in the window as engine 480 belched black smoke, working hard to pull the 14 cars up the canyon grade. The polished rods and levers of the ''monkey works'' attached to the wheels flashed their crazy motion in the sun only to disappear around yet another curve.

Getting more comfortable, the boy took a rock out of his pocket and looked at it closely. Black and yellow minerals sparkled in the white quartz matrix. An old gentleman came up the aisle, knees bent, his waist like a gimbal; he had the gait of an old sailor on ship's deck. He sat down across from the hiker who was still studying the rock.

''Been doin' a little prospectin' son?'' the old gent said.

''Er, well not really. Just camping mostly. Here, do you know what's in it?''

He gave the old timer the rock, who, furrowing his brow and turning it over in this thick hands, gave it the close eye of a jeweler inspecting a diamond.

''An interesting specimen that one is,'' remarked the gent ''I'd say you've been up around Whitehead Peak, eh?''

Surprised, the boy admitted he had found it near there.

''What's in it? Does it have any gold?'' he asked.

''Well, I don't have a glass on me, but these specks laying along the zinc may be telluride gold.''

The boy looked at it, barely detecting the specks.

''Well, how do I know for sure?'' he asked.

''There's still an assay office in Silverton, and a good bit of mining too, not like in the old days, but ten or twenty million in gold a year is nothing to sneeze at, even today. Used to haul all that out by train, but today this line carries tourists, like yourself, not gold. Weren't fer that, this old car'd be a chicken coop in Bayfield, I bet.''

''Really? It looks like it's in such good shape.''

The gent smiled, ''Well, that's 'cause it's been restored better than new in the car shops in Durango. Back in the forties the Rio Grande couldn't get rid of this old junk fast enough. Had some hot-shots in Denver who wanted a modern railroad, not the old teakettle stuff, and narrow-gauge to boot.''

''What do you mean by narrow-gauge, exactly?''

''Did you notice everything's a bit smaller on this train? It's not an illusion. The rails, see, are only three feet wide instead of four feet eight and a half inches like on mainline roads. You see, these tight curves and narrow canyons would be impossible for a broad-gauge line, so they built these narrow-gauge outfits all through the Colorado Rockies.

''There were lines all over. Durango had four. The 'mainline' east over Cumbres Pass to Alamosa, the Farmington Branch, the Silverton Branch, and the Rio Grande Southern west then north through Rico, Telluride and Ridgway, where it hit the D&RGW again. Called it the Narrow-Gauge Circle. Hauled gold, silver and vanadium ores, oil, lumber and sheep, out; supplies, hardware, dynamite and even new automobiles, in. Yep, it took the narrow-gauge to bring those autos in, then those same autos turn around and take our business away!

''Luckily tourists and rail buffs discovered the Silverton in the late fifties so this forty-five miles of line was saved, along with sixty-four miles of the Cumbres and Toltec line from Chama, New Mexico to Antonito, Colorado. Only a hundred-ten miles left from the twelve-hundred around in 1883.''

''Wow, that's quite a change,'' admitted the boy. ''When did they build this line? Was it the Rio Grande who did?''

''Well sir, the Denver and Rio Grande started in 1871 to build south to Mexico. In 1878 rich silver and gold was found in Leadville, and three lines raced to build west, into the mountains, first. The Santa Fe and Rio Grande both tried to build up the narrow Royal Gorge of the Arkansas River, but there was only room for one line. The Santa Fe brought in Bat Masterson and some gunmen from Dodge City, Kansas, but the Rio Grande didn't just sit there. General William J. Palmer, an ex-Union general, ran the Rio Grande, and he covered the right-of-way with barricades and forts armed with sharpshooters. The Santa Fe, however, beat the Rio Grande in court. Palmer learned his lesson, and lost no time building

Dell A. McCoy Photograph

Number 481, which never saw service on the
Silverton branch under D&RGW management, hauls
passengers out of Durango along the line which had
been improved in order to handle its weight.

to all of the other silver boom towns, and Silverton
was the biggest in the San Juans. So the San Juan
Extension was built, which got to Durango in 1881,
and Silverton in 1882.''

''Does the Denver and Rio Grande still own the
Durango-Silverton?''

''No, they sold it in 1981 to Charles Bradshaw, a
millionaire who loved this train so much, he bought
it. He's spent millions fixing it up. Like our engine,
Number 480. She was an old freight hog that hadn't
run since the early sixties, when they stopped the
long pipe trains to the oil fields in Farmington. Same

with 481 and 497, both newly restored. He expanded
the roundhouse and shops in Durango, too, and rebuilt all the cars. Runs more trains as well, so folks
won't be disappointed and miss the ride like they
used to.''

''Well, I guess I missed a lot of the ride myself,''
remarked the hiker, ''since I got on at Elk Park. Is
the train always in this deep canyon?''

''No son, sometimes it's even deeper!'', the old
timer chuckled, '''course it starts in Durango, which
is in a broad valley. General Palmer founded the
town when the railroad got there, named it after

Dell A. McCoy Photograph

D&SNG passenger train smokes its way upgrade through the narrows of the Animas River Canyon just below Silverton.

120

Richard A. Bell Photograph

ABOVE: A double header, with Number 476 and Number 478 pulling upgrade, rolls past the water tank at Hermosa.

Locomotive Number 473 drifts downgrade, as Number 478 waits to continue its upgrade haul, at the siding below Hermosa.

Richard A. Bell Photograph

Dell A. McCoy Photograph

Number 497, formerly a standard-gauge locomotive and the largest owned by the Durango &
Silverton, approaches the Rockwood ledge on its trip
toward Silverton.

Durango, Mexico. Since Palmer had never made it to
the real Durango, he just started his own! Durango
was the smelter town for processing the ores. With
the nearby coal mines, it was cheaper to bring the
ore down to the smelter, than haul the bulky coal up
to the Silverton mines. The smelter closed in 1932,
and only the tall brick smokestack remains today. By
the seventies skiing, resorts and of course the train
has made Durango a pretty fancy place, indeed.

"Back in the forties, the Silverton train ran three
days a week, with only a couple of coaches and boxcars full of dynamite for the Shenandoah-Dives
Mine, which was the largest mine in the district.
Third biggest silver mine in Colorado! It was run by
an engineer with a degree in Philosophy! Sounds
funny now, but old Pappa Chase made money when
no one else could, then or now.

"But I'm gettin' derailed here. Anyway, once you
leave Durango, the train heads up the fertile, wide
valley to Hermosa. Good farmlands down there,
used to be dairy farms all along making sweet milk
out of the hay down in the 'sloos. Halfway up was
Trimble Hot Springs Resort, said to be an old Ute
Indian cure spot. Special trains ran there in the old
days, it was so popular, but now it's gone.

"Hermosa is where one of the old water towers

stands. Bradshaw made it the new track gang headquarters. There is a $100,000 track fixin' machine
that does the work of twenty men the old way, and
makes for a safer and smoother ride. Six miles of
new rail, and 40,000 new ties have been put in since
1981.

"Now that's progress!

"Past Hermosa the train hits steep grades, climbing out of the valley along the huge white sandstone
Hermosa Cliffs. The engine is about fifteen feet
higher than the caboose on that hill! Below is
Baker's Bridge, where Captain Baker and his
pioneer prospectors camped in 1861. Rockwood is
the next station, then you really hold onto your
seat!"

"Why, what happens then?" asked the bewilder-
ed boy.

"The river has dropped over four-hundred feet
below the track, and you're in the Animas Gorge!
It's so narrow that they had to hang from ropes to cut
the roadbed out of the solid red granite cliff. You can
still see the blasting craters from the black powder
explosions. The shelf is so skinny if you spit out the
window you'd hit the river, and the curve is so tight
you can read the engineer's watch from the last
car!"

"Awe, come on, you're pulling my leg."

"Well, maybe just a little," the old timer grinned.
"Anyway, after the gorge you cross the river on the
high trestle, and get beside it again, at the town of
Tacoma. Population 17, more or less, says the sign.
It's a power plant and a few houses. Water comes
down a flume from Electra Lake, a thousand feet
above. The tracks above here got washed out in
1911, and again in 1970. You can still see old rail and
junk in the river along the way. Makes a fisherman
pretty mad when he pulls in a big one, only to find
it's an old spike!"

"Where do the fishermen come from?"

"Oh, the next stop is 'Ah Wilderness', a guest
ranch in the canyon, along with Tall Timber Resort a
mile farther up. Only way in or out is by the narrow-
gauge. Once I saw the crew pick up a dog here, and
stop in Tacoma to send him home. 'Course they told
the dispatcher they'd stopped to check the brakes.
Couldn't have charged the poor lost dog for a ride,
now could they?

"The canyon is really pretty here. Quaky trees,
meadows of wild flowers and all that. At Cascade
Canyon a turn-around wye was built for the winter
runs. They used to shut down in the winter, but old
Charlie Bradshaw runs the train year round, every
day but Christmas and New Years, even if its got no
paying passengers! Then the valley gets a bit
narrow, and the mountains start to tower overhead.
A couple of foot bridges cross the river to get into the
wilderness area. Then comes Needleton, named
after the Needle Mountains surrounding the train. It
was an old stage road stop. The train has to stop here
for water, at another old tank. These engines use
some fifteen thousand gallons of water, and six tons

of coal to make the ninety mile round trip. And that coal has to be shoveled by hand! Shoveling coal, keeping the water up and watching the track keep a fireman as busy as a monkey. Past Needleton is where the slides really start.''

"Slides? You mean snow-slides?'' asked the boy.

"Yep. Run down narrow chutes three-thousand feet above the tracks, and often go right across the river and up the other side! Even dams the river up for a few hours 'til it cuts through again. Some of those slides are seventy-five feet deep on the tracks. In the old days it was easier to tunnel through the snow than to dig it out. Might stay there 'til August in that dark canyon. Now, they have Cats to plow out the line every spring. The canyon is over four-thousand feet deep here, until it finally widens out again into ...''

"Into Elk Park,'' the boy interrupted with a smile, "where I got on.''

"Hey, that's some pretty good geography son. You'll make a good prospector with that head of yours. Look out there, we're just about to Silverton now.''

The old timer pointed to a broad valley ahead, known as a park in these parts; Bakers Park, where Silverton lies.

"Look at that mine! What mine is that?'' exclaimed the boy as he looked out the coach window.

Across from the train was a tunnel cut into the five-hundred foot, sheer gray cliff. A string of little yellow ore cars sat on a wooden trestle above the ore bins.

"Oh, that's the Pittsburgh Tunnel of the old Champion Mine, over a mile long in the mountain. It was an old silver and gold mine that's been fixed up recently to tap the veins in Sultan Mountain above.''

Suddenly the train crossed a low steel trestle over Mineral Creek, and the engine let out a long cry of its whistle to announce its presence in the old mining camp. The railroad yards are still decorated with ore loading tipples and gondola cars waiting as if to load up with rich silver ores for the trip to the smelter. Reaching the ancient yellow and brown depot, the station master pulled a gold watch out of his vest and gave the engineer the highball sign. On time again! Slowing, the train entered the curve on Twelfth Street, and ran into town to stop, its brass bell clanging at Blair Street.

Another train sat lazily on the siding waiting for its return load of passengers.

The old timer and the boy got off and sauntered up the street.

"Gosh, this ride was great, and I really liked your stories. Now where is that assay office so I can find out if I found gold?''

The old timer pointed down the street, past the old saloons and gambling joints of the boom days, to a faded, old false-front building.

"Remember son,'' said the old man with a twinkle, "they say gold is where you find it, but I think what you find in life—that's the real gold.''

The boy looked back at the old engine, sitting contented, with steam wisping out of the "snifter" ports, and thought he knew what the old timer meant.

Locomotive Number 473 crosses the steel bridge below Electra Lake on its way north.

Approaching the end of its upgrade struggle, Number 473 draws close to the Snowshed slide in the Animas River canyon below Silverton.

A work extra watches the 10 a.m. "San Juan Express" pass as it rolls into Silverton.

Heading down the canyon from Silverton, Number 476 is accompanied by the green waters of the Animas River.

Even William H. Jackson came to Leadville to photograph the Ice Palace. This print is from one of several glass plate negatives he exposed.

Colorado's 1859 gold rush brought large numbers of people into the Pikes Peak country for the first time. Available statistics suggest that the gold-seekers and those who followed them far outnumbered all of the combined fur trappers, official explorers, military expeditions and early pleasure-seekers who entered present Colorado prior to the gold rush. Those who came to seek their fortunes in the mines gravitated mostly to Clear Creek and Gilpin Counties. That same year gold was also located in today's Boulder County and another, but smaller, rush of miners settled around the Gold Hill district. Some prospectors who considered the front range towns too crowded made their way across the Continental Divide to South Park. There they built towns like Hamilton, Tarryall, Fairplay and Buckskin Joe.

But there were other more adventuresome souls who trespassed onto Ute hunting lands in their reckless search for gold. They entered the broad, open upper Arkansas Valley and made a strike on April 25, 1859. About 25 miles above Kelly's Bar they found gold bearing gravel. The word spread like measels in the proverbial kindergarten. Perhaps because so many disappointed Californians participated in the excitement, the area soon assumed the name of California Gulch. Another version of the story involves a prospector named Abe Lee who scooped up a rich pan of placer gravel and loudly claimed that he had "all of California" there in his pan. Either way the name became firmly entrenched in common usage and survives today.

Not far above the site of Lee's discovery a ramshackle collection of tents, brush covered caves, wagons and log cabins sprang up. Probably because

gold was the prevailing metal found there they kited the Spanish word for it and called their town Oro City. Since formal government did not exist in the area at that time other names were used too. Among them were Sacramento City, Slabtown and Boughtown, but eventually the Oro City name prevailed. An early report describes how these various habitations extended for six miles in a line down the valley to the later site of Malta.

Because the upper Arkansas Valley exceeds 10,000 feet of elevation the nights were cold. Those who lacked the previously described shelters slept on the ground under wooden packing crates, or they crawled into outhouses to escape the bone-chilling cold. Entrepreneurs who erected a circus tent were able to clear $1,000 nightly by selling sleeping spaces on the ground at $1 each.

In a very short time gamblers and prostitutes arrived. They operated their own business ventures out of canvas-topped "cat wagons", although the former usually brought larger portable shelters. Oro City's first saloons also dispensed their libations from tents. When preachers arrived to safeguard the morals of the Argonauts, they often preached in tent saloons as there were few other available spaces as yet. Some gamblers set up their equipment along the trails to the better diggings to assure that the weight of the gold would not impede the miner's walk down to his humble abode.

Among the earliest arrivals were Augusta and Horace A.W. Tabor who had made the journey from Denver in just three months. From Denver the Tabors moved south along the Front Range to Ute Pass, at the edge of today's Manitou Springs. This ancient Indian hunting trail took them across the first range to Trout Creek Pass in the lower end of South

Leadville,

Park. Augusta's diary describes how they widened and shored up the old path in order to get their wagon through. From the Trout Creek crossing they entered the Arkansas Valley and were able to follow the river up to their destination. Shortly after their arrival, Augusta was described as being "the only family type woman in California Gulch." At first the Tabors supported themselves by taking in boarders, and Augusta served meals. By July of 1860 log structures had begun to replace the ruder accommodations.

By 1861 there were an estimated 10,000 persons in the gulch. Since most of the claims were above the town, water was used and re-used until it assumed a thick muddy consistency as it flowed through Oro City. Later a twelve mile long wooden trough was built to bring water to the residents. Oro City lasted for approximately three years despite a climate that restricted mining to the warmer months. For rather obvious reasons the life of most placer camps is short. As the richer gold deposits were exhausted, people began to move away. But they left too soon, unable to foresee what was about to occur.

Another miner named Charles Mullen located the rich Printer Boy Mine in 1868. His find was a mere three miles above Oro City. What he had found was gold in the form of nuggets and wire. In their haste to get settled near the latest bonanza, the miners picked up the smaller cabins from Oro City and disassembled the larger structures. Most surface buildings were loaded onto flatbed wagons and hauled up to the vicinity of the Printer Boy. There a second community came to life. And what name did they choose to call it? Oro City of course. So there were two Oro Citys just three miles apart in California Gulch. The Tabors moved up, too and opened a store, restaurant, bakery and express service from the new town to Denver. Until the trails became roads two weeks were required for the round trip.

An occasional band of Utes, usually intoxicated, tried unsuccessfully to drive the intruders out. Such a band once attacked Stringtown, a suburb located below the mouth of California Gulch. Although restive and resentful of the invasion of their cherished hunting ground, when sober they kept their distance. The new gold boom lasted less than three years, but many residents stayed on anyway. Among those who remained were the Tabors. He was now 40 years old. For nearly a decade they stayed on in their cabin at the almost forgotten camp.

There was still a post office at Oro City as late as 1901, but the decline had started back in the 1870s. One factor contributing to the downfall was the unwieldiness of mining operations. A thick, heavy black sand plugged up the miners' sluice boxes.

Only later did a more perceptive metallurgist figure out that this substance was actually carbonate of lead and very rich in silver. Although it was gold that had first attracted people to the upper Arkansas Valley, it was silver that would bring it lasting fame as one of the West's greatest and most lawless mining camps.

In 1878 William "Uncle Billy" Stevens and his partner Alvinus B. Wood figured out the secret of the heavy black sands. Wood's tests showed that each ton of the stuff carried as much as 40 ounces of silver. Wood stayed on but Stevens left the gulch in the spring of 1880 with $500, 239 pounds of Oro City gold and an unstipulated quantity of silver.

Evelyn and Robert L. Brown Collection

In previous years silver had been mined primarily as a by-product. But that was before the Republican Party discovered that it needed the votes of the western silver states to stay in power. To curry their favor Congress passed two pieces of legislation to artificially shore up the price of the white metal. First to come was the Bland-Allison Act which boosted the price but introduced a quota. The second bill was the Sherman Silver Purchase Act which removed the quota and required the Treasury to buy all of the silver mined in America, and at an inflated price that was unrealistic in terms of the price in the rest of the world. Under this law, between 1879 and 1889, $82,000,000 in silver was mined and shipped from Leadville.

When word of silver in Colorado reached the East the predicted rush followed. Leadville was founded in 1877 and incorporated as a city in 1888. In size it was second only to Denver. Lake County grew from a

Colorado's Cloud City

by Robert L. Brown   127

ABOVE: At the Oro City site only matchstick timbers remain as evidence of the town that was once here.

BELOW: William H. Jackson exposed this plate of the second Oro City near the Printer Boy Mine in California Gulch.

ABOVE: From the same angle, this color view looks across Leadville toward the same peaks of the Sawatch Range.

BELOW: Railroad photographer George Beam took this photograph of booming Leadville. Mount Massive is in the center, and Mount Elbert is on the left.

population of 500 to 24,000 by the time the census of 1880 was taken. The same count listed four banks, 31 restaurants, 17 barber shops, the Tabor Grand Opera House, five churches and a whopping 249 saloons at Leadville!

People came up the valley from more than 30 states and from 11 foreign countries. In the absence of firm statistics we can only guess at the number who participated in the rush of 1878-79. The most conservative guess was 10,000, while the most generous suggestion was 40,000, but today nobody is quite sure. They arrived too quickly for the new town to house them or for laws to be written. Hotels, such as they were, could not accommodate even those who were able to afford their ridiculous prices. Soon there were flophouses where one could crawl into a tiered wooden bunk with a total stranger for 50c a night. There you could shiver through an eight hour shift under an unwashed blanket until hustled rudely out by the proprietor to make room for the next victim. If a flophouse didn't suit your tastes you could visit a saloon and drink all night. This provided shelter and escape from the ever-present cold.

Other miners paid to sleep on the floors of gambling emporiums, saloons, warehouses or stables. But some of the more devious minds contrived a more interesting solution. At dinner time they would enter one of the tonier restaurants, order the most expensive meal on the menu and then refuse to pay. When the police were called the "dead beat" was able to spend the night in a warm jail cell at no cost. Restaurant owners countered with a trip to Denver where they hired out-of-work Irishmen as bouncers. By 1879 the Trans-continental railroad was finished and many Irish "gandy dancers" had gravitated to Denver. So when a customer refused to settle his tab the Irishmen threw him into the street and walloped the living bejabers out of him with his shelaleigh. Only then would the authorities be summoned to haul the grateful victim off to jail. Needless to say, this curbed the practice of free meals followed by a semi-comfortable night in the slammer.

Efforts to collect taxes and assessments were hooted down and Leadville lacked even the money to remove street refuse or to pay a police force. Why accept law enforcement work in a bankrupt town when better paying jobs were available in the mines? Because law enforcement was inadequate, crime flourished. Armed hoodlums once seized and held the Presbyterian Church while other lot jumpers openly walked the streets. On two occasions thugs tried to tear down St. Vincents Hospital. Father Robinson armed himself and about a hundred volunteers. In later years Robinson admitted to carrying a revolver under his priestly raiments, "as did everyone else in Leadville." Finally a vigilante committee got their act together, marched some of the lawless element out of town at gunpoint and threatened the rest with the wrath of the "Local Uplift Society" unless they were out of town within ten days.

Called the "Cloud City," Leadville enjoys the distinction of being the highest incorporated city in America. Its elevation is 10,152 feet above sea level. Both of Colorado's highest mountains, 14,421 foot Mount Massive and 14,433 foot Mount Elbert are visible from Harrison Avenue, the principal street through the city. Living at such an elevation dictated some frustrating adjustments for the pioneers. Eastern recipe books had to be changed, it took longer to boil water and there was less oxygen in the air. Even walking up a flight of stairs was tiring. Residents claimed only two seasons: three months of summer and nine of winter. If a person died in winter it required dynamite to excavate the grave. The explosions broke windows, cracked walls and shook dishes out of cupboards. Public indignation curbed the practice. One enterprising undertaker dug a series of graves in summer for winter sale, at a seasonal mark-up of course.

Because of the distance from sources of supply, groceries sold at four times the Denver prices. Pneumonia, the scourge of most high altitude towns, was rampant. Leadville authorities buried the victims at night lest the toll become known and slow down the rush. One source describes a "dead cart" patterned after those used in Europe during the black plague. To say the least, life in the upper Arkansas Valley was different.

Religion came early to Leadville. Rev. John L. "Father" Dyer, most energetic of the early circuit-riding clergy, preached regularly in the city. Until churches could be built, services were held on street corners, in homes or in larger saloons. Rev. Thomas Uzzell was typical of Leadville's church men. He understood the miner's way of life and sometimes carried his message into the worst places. He could brawl with the best of them to gain attention and respect. Uzzell also understood instant conversion. He first "saw the light" at a Methodist tent revival back in Illinois where he and his brothers had gone to heckle the parson and shoot peas at the worshipers when heads were bowed. Rev. Uzzell built Leadville's very first church. Later there were Episcopal, Baptist, Congregational, Campbellite and Catholic churches there.

Two railroad companies recognized the importance of the Leadville traffic and laid tracks to the city. Following a bitter fight with the Atchison, Topeka and Santa Fe over access to the Royal Gorge, the Denver and Rio Grande entered the city in 1880. The occasion was considered to be of such importance that President Grant and hs family came west to ride the first train. Harrison Avenue was decorated with evergreens and patriotic bunting, and a parade honored both the railroad and the distinguished guests. That evening the Grants attended a performance in their honor at the Tabor Opera House as guests of Mr. and Mrs. H.A.W. Tabor.

Leadville's second railroad was the Denver, South Park and Pacific. Since it was a narrow gauge it was built through the mountains. By 1878 its tracks had

State Street was Leadville's rowdiest. It was lined with saloons, gambling dens and brothels. The Theatre Comique appears at the left. Mount Massive is seen at the end of the street. A fire destroyed nearly all of these buildings.

been laid through the canyon of the South Platte River to Bailey. It crossed Kenosha Pass to Como and Boreas and Fremont Passes to reach Leadville in 1884.

Aside from the Tabors, quite a number of well known people came to be associated with Leadville. Dow of Dow-Jones was there. Meyer Guggenheim made a fortune in smelting. David May came up from Irwin to open his May Company department store. Margaret Tobin Brown, the fabled "Unsinkable Molly," was married to and subsequently divorced from a Leadville miner. Charles Vivian, founder of the Fraternal Order of Elks, charmed local audiences with his vocal rendition of "10,000 Miles Away." After Oscar Wilde was expelled from his native England for homosexual activities he made a lecture tour of America. When he played Leadville a curious crowd packed the hall to observe his "aestheticism." Eddie Foy performed at the Theatre Comique on State Street and married Rose Howland, a singer there. Denver's Claude Boettcher made a fortune at Leadville, started the Portland Cement Company and Boettcher and Company on Denver's 17th Street. His mansion is now home to Colorado's governor. On the seamier side Bat Masterson and "Doc" Holliday were no strangers to the city. Jefferson Randolph "Soapy" Smith conducted his games of chance there until he moved to greener pastures at Creede.

Leadville spent $120,000 building an Ice Palace in the winter of 1895-96. It stood on a vacant lot between 7th and 8th Streets. 5,000 tons of two by five foot blocks of ice were stacked against a wooden frame interior. It measured 450 feet in length by 350 feet wide. Ninety foot-high towers adorned its corners. A 90 x 180 foot skating rink, two ballrooms with pine floors, a restaurant and an exhibit hall were inside. The walls of the exhibit hall consisted of Colorado products frozen into the blocks of ice. There were cuts of beef, Coors beer, vegetables and ore specimens. At night. colored spotlights played across its walls. It opened on New Year's Day with a parade, even though the temperature was eight below zero. Admission cost 50c, and the railroads operated special excursion trains to visit the "Crystal Carnival." By June it had mostly melted away, and the stunt was never repeated.

By the time the Ice Palace was constructed, the city's best days were over. The decade between 1879 and 1889 was the most prosperous time. Then in 1893 the repeal of the Sherman Silver Purchase Act caused the price of silver to plummet. The repeal was sought by President Cleveland to save our international credit, but it was a disaster for all of the Western silver producing states. Here in Colorado the repeal was called the "Crime of 1893."

Today Leadville is on the National Register of Historic Sites. The Tabor Grand Opera House still stands as does the Tabor Grand Hotel, now called the Vendome. In the gulches to the east of the town one may visit Tabor's Matchless Mine, see Iron, Fryer and Carbonate Hills and explore many of the once rich mines that made Leadville one of the West's greatest and most unique silver camps.

ABOVE: Blue-gray cinder deposits mark the same railroad grade seen in the Beam picture. Also note the same church spire and roads that came down from the hill at the right.

BELOW: While George Beam was in Leadville, he made this picture from the east end of Eighth Street. Mount Massive is in the distance.

From the identical vantage point, here was Harrison Avenue during the summer of 1984.

BELOW: Early Leadville was nearly devoid of trees. This view looks south down Harrison Avenue. The Tabor Grand Hotel and the Court House appear on the right.

Steven J. Meyers Photograph

Powder Heaven, Ski To

It's an old question, and all of us who have lived in small mountain towns have heard it. Some of us resent it, some of us don't listen, and some of us just smile. "What do you do in the winter?" There are many ways to answer the question, some truthful, some not so. "It's a good time to catch up on your reading." "Why do you think our birth rate is so high?" If the truth were told, however, it is the time of year some of us await most anxiously.

Spring is a time of rebirth, and in many parts of the country a gentle time of rekindling. In the mountains it is dominated by mud, and cold, wet weather. Summer is too short, and too glorious for words. It is a time for doing the things which need to be done, housepainting, plumbing, woodgathering, and for wonderful days of hiking, climbing and fishing in the hot sun. Fall can be long or short depending on the year, and it too is glorious. The mountains are ablaze with color and the air becomes crisp and delicious much like the apples which appear at the same time. For the person who loves winter these signs stir the blood because they mean only one thing: soon snow will begin to fall and the mountains will be draped in the soft wrap of one of nature's finest gifts, powder snow.

Skiing in powder snow is an addiction not unlike other addictions, but unlike most others it is neither fattening nor bad for your health. As with other addictions there exist fierce loyalties, and many are the "friendly" discussions involving the character of one's chosen obsession. Powder skiers will argue with great conviction about the quality of their favorite snow, and the beauty of their favorite places; how much more deeply rooted in the psyche these arguments become when they spring from perceptions about your home it is difficult to say, but no powder lover is more fiercely loyal than a local. I am no exception.

Little Cottonwood Canyon in the Wasatch Mountains of Utah has legendary snow which has made the ski area of Alta justly famous. A very short way down the canyon is Snowbird which draws a devoted breed of powder hound. These two areas are separated by a narrow ridge, and to many would appear to be virtually the same ski area, but powder connoisseurs are quick to point out that the snow at the two places is just not the same. Old time powder lovers will ski Alta in preference to the flashier Snowbird because, as they say, "the snow is better." Many insist that Alta snow is the best in the world, and few will argue. Some of those few live in the Tetons of Wyoming. Some are around Sun Valley in Idaho. This particular member of that group of dissenters lives in the San Juan Mountains of southwestern Colorado, and I would take San Juan snow over anything I have ever skied.

Just what it is that makes San Juan powder so special is difficult to say. A common misconception is that great powder is the lightest powder, or more accurately, the snow with the least density. In low density snow there is less water for a given volume of snow, and it seems to have the consistency of goose down. While it is true that low density snow skis better than the infamous Sierra Cement, or the dense, wet snow of the Cascades in the Northwest, the extreme low density snow of, say, Alaska, usually makes for poor skiing because it fails to float the skis. A skier in this snow simply drops out of sight. What is needed is an optimum density, lightness with body. If you are beginning to think that you took a wrong turn and have arrived at a wine tasting, your perception is not too far from correct. With snow, similar fine distinctions exist. San Juan powder, like powder everywhere, varies from storm to storm, and from day to day, but often, more often than anywhere else I have skied, it has this wonderful quality of lightness with body.

Beyond the snow, however, there are other critical elements. Skiing is a total experience, and snow, while a very important part of that experience is certainly not the only factor. Powder skiing is an aesthetic as well as athletic activity, and nowhere in the world is there more sheer beauty than in the San Juans. Skiable terrain is surrounded by breathtaking vistas filled with jagged peaks, intimate scenes of wooded beauty and the joyous companionship of wildlife. Finally, there is the San Juan's ace in the hole: weather. Nowhere else is there the marvelous synchronicity of latitude, altitude and proximity to desert which exist here. The Wasatch range in Utah gets regular dumps of wonderful snow, but days there are cold by San Juan standards, and skiing there can be a bone chilling affair. The Sangre de Cristo range near Taos, New Mexico is relatively warm, but its snow is highly erratic and unpredictable. The San Juans, perfectly situated between them get regular, consistently excellent snow, and between storms there are what can only be called "San Juan Days", days of magnificent blue skies

uring In The San Juans

by Steven J. Meyers

Pidgeon Peak, nearly 14,000 feet high, rises above the Animas River Valley in the southern San Juans between Durango and Silverton.

A lone ski tourer finds solitude and beauty along South Mineral Creek just north of Silverton.

ABOVE: A blanket of fresh snow covers the beautiful and easily skied terrain on Molas Pass just south of Silverton.

Anyone travelling in avalanche country should carry the equipment necessary for rescue in the event of avalanche. More important, however, is the knowledge to use it effectively, and to avoid problems in the first place. Each skier should carry a shovel, extra clothing and food, as well as a device for locating buried skiers. An avalanche transceiver, like the one pictured here, may be expensive, but is worth its weight in gold when needed.

137

and almost balmy breezes which occur regularly throughout the winter. These are days made for skiing the abundant powder.

Equipment for skiing the backcountry has changed a great deal in the decades since skiing hit Colorado. There was a time when the same pair of skis you wore up the lift served you well for skiing beyond the ski area boundaries as well. If it was powder you craved, all you had to do was plane down the tips of your wooden downhill skis until they "waved at you like cobras" from the snow, hike up your favorite mountain in your relatively soft leather boots, then turn around and head down for the time of your life. Technology and the growth in popularity of Nordic style equipment have changed all of that, and the days of one-pair-can-do-everything skis have long since vanished. Specialty skis have proliferated to the point of absurdity, and the novice powder skier might find the choices confusing, but for backcountry skiing the complexity is greatly reduced. The choice boils down to two: Nordic touring and alpine touring.

Nordic touring equipment, which appears to have replaced alpine touring gear to a very large extent, is characterized by lightness and comfort. The skis are long and narrow, the boots are leather and relatively flexible, and the three pin binding which attaches the toe of the boot to the ski is uncomplicated and allows for great freedom of motion. This equipment is less tiring to use than alpine touring gear while hiking and climbing and in its simpler forms also less expensive.

Alpine touring gear is similar to the equipment you see at downhill ski areas. The skis are considerably wider than Nordic skis, and also heavier. The boots are usually constructed from rigid plastic, and the bindings, while allowing a free heel for climbing, have a lock-down heel for descents.

Alpine touring equipment, with the wider ski, rigid boot and locked heel binding used to be the choice for steep, difficult and icy descents. It was also considered better for hard to ski snow conditions such as wind slab, sun crust and breakable crust. Nordic backcountry gear has undergone considerable refinement since touring skis first became popular, and metal edges, stiffer boots, and stronger bindings have eliminated the advantages of alpine gear in all but the most extreme conditions. The technological improvements, however, have not been one sided. Alpine touring skis are lighter than they used to be, and a new generation of ski-mountaineering boots is both lighter and more comfortable than the downhill boot we once fit into alpine touring bindings.

Making turns with the two different types of skis quickly demonstrates their differences. It is possible to ski Nordic equipment with the same technique used for alpine skis, but most Nordic skiers prefer to use the telemark turn. This graceful turn, once thought an extinct relic of ski history, has been re-invented, and is enjoying something of a renaissance. A telemark turn is accomplished by sliding the leg opposite the direction you wish to turn forward, placing much of your weight on the advanced ski, and angling the ski against the snow by turning the advanced knee inward as the foot steers in the direction of the turn. The rear ski follows as if you were skiing on a single, long, articulated ski. Turns are linked by alternately sliding the skis forward and, well, turning. The free heel of the Nordic binding makes this possible, and the extension of the ski platform forward and back makes the telemark position extremely stable in situations of abrupt speed change. Telemarks feel great dropping over drifts and rolls. Alpine touring skis can be telemarked if the heels are not locked down, but are generally skied parallel. Parallel skiing in powder, especially on a steep slope, is a very special feeling. The parallel turn widens the base of support laterally (as opposed to longitudinally as in the telemark), and is therefore far more stable from side to side. There is a flow and rhythm in skiing powder parallel which allows you to play with the snow and gravity in a way not really possible with the telemark. As with everything else in skiing, the final choice is one of temperament and aesthetics. The grace and elegance of telemarks, the lightness of Nordic gear, versus the play and flow of alpine equipment. The choice is yours; either way you win.

Powder is the blessing of winter, and the steep slopes of the San Juans are the perfect vehicle for skiing it. Unfortunately, powder snow and steep slopes, mixed with skiers, are also the perfect vehicle for avalanches. No one who has lived in, or travelled through the San Juans in winter can remain unimpressed with an avalanche's power. Everywhere there is evidence of what they can do. Huge mounds of deposition sit on valley floors. Highways pass through deep cuts in their debris. Large trees, hundreds of years old, lie in the debris shattered like straw. If an avalanche can uproot, transport, and reduce to splinters a hundred foot pine tree, imagine what one might do to a skier! No one skiing in the backcountry should venture out without the knowledge and equipment necessary to deal with this very real and present hazard.

Avalanche awareness and training come about in several ways. One is to spend time skiing with those who have experience, listening to what they teach about snow, and learning to see what they see. Another way to learn about avalanche hazard and how to deal with it is to attend an avalanche training course. Perhaps the best method of all is to combine the two approaches. Often people who presume to know a great deal about recognizing danger and avoiding hazard know very little. Having some expert input might help you decide whom it would be safe to ski with, and whom to leave in the bar talking about it.

Once knowledge is gained, and experienced partners found, never venture into avalanche terrain without the equipment to effect a rescue should all of your training in hazard avoidance somehow manage to fail you. Be prepared for other hazards as well. Injuries, hypothermia and frostbite can all be deadly, and can all be encountered while skiing. Once again, be prepared, go with people who are knowledgable, and learn as much as you can. Skiing should be fun, not an exercise in survival.

The morning comes quickly, and there is excitement in the air. Last night a friend called to say he had the day off, that he'd heard the snow was great, the forecast was clear and mild, and how would I like to try the powder up on Red Mountain Pass? Slowly creeping down from the summits of the peaks surrounding home, the glow of the sun warms my heart and fires my expectations. My boots sit by the woodstove, my skis with climbing skins attached are out in the snow by the front door, and my breakfast stares me in the face. I eat it, but I don't really taste it. My mind is filled with thoughts of crisp air, white peaks, good friends, and powder.

The horn honks and I'm off with my gear to jump into the pickup. Having reached the valley floor, the sun streams in through the windows warming my face. At Chattanooga we stop to pick up a friend and head up the pass. Twenty minutes from home, everyone together, skis on, we begin the climb up to MacMillan Peak. Tentative probes of the ski poles confirm our hopes: the powder is excellent. We ski through the woods silently, feeling the snow, smelling the air, watching the clouds and critters. An Ermine dives over a bank to avoid us. The record in the snow tells a tale about a ground squirrel's last battle with a hawk. We continue upward.

At timberline the sun comes into its full glory, and the sky is a shade of blue too deep to be real, except that it is. Above us is the peak. Around us the snow. We stop to dig a pit, and assured that the snow is reasonably stable we continue upward. From both sides of the ridge we ascend the world falls away and our stomachs lift and fall in sympathy with our anticipated feelings, the vertigo induced by the knowledge that we will soon find ourselves floating, flying, swooping down through it. At the summit we find no wind, and the view each of us has seen before, but will never get used to. From here the world is filled with light. An infinite sea of mountains surrounds us. We are small. We are large. We are happy.

We stop long enough to stow our climbing skins, don parkas and eat some cheese and crackers. Light hearted insults which belie our deep mutual respect and affection are tossed about. "You learned how to ski yet?" "Want me to carry you down?" And inevitably, "Yep, just another crummy day in paradise".

Food stashed, canteens drained, and bindings fastened we turn to leave the summit and ski down.

I don't think I'll try to describe the trip down. Nothing, I fear, would do it justice. Was it like flying? Were we able to be eagles for just a little while? Or better, were we able to soar like the beings we truly are, freed from petty concerns, in touch with something so real and immediate that nothing else could intrude?

All that and more.

Another crummy day in paradise.

American history is framed in the notion of frontier. Perhaps it is a temperamental residue, the genetic gift of those who came here from Europe filled with expectation, hope and myths about what the land would be. Whatever its source, that sense of expectation, a desire to see what lies beyond the next green pasture, across the next river, over the next range of mountains has characterized our settlement, our growth, and is now a major component of our national psyche.

To a very large extent we have settled the areas which once filled us with wonder, and our familiarity with them has removed them from the category of frontier. It is hard to believe that at one time Pennsylvania was considered the uttermost west. Now, even though it is filled with natural beauty, many of us dismiss it as another of those eastern industrial states. For those surrounded by evidence of civilization the notion of frontier is particularly precious. For many, images of the west still involve rugged mountains and a rugged life to match. State names like Alaska, Oregon, Idaho and Colorado in particular evoke images of beauty and wildness. Those of us who live in these states, however, are far more likely to be familiar with the civilized reality of their towns and cities than the primitive wildness of their backcountry. Still, even with the jaded familiarity residence in such a place brings, there is romance and excitement in the mentioning of mythical frontier, in the names of places which have not ceased to fill us with expectation and wonder. For the Coloradan the San Juans are such a place.

About ten years ago I lived in Denver, held a job, and tried in my spare time to get into the mountains as much as possible. My friends and associates included a number of like minded individuals, and much city time was spent talking about our favorite places. Some spoke about the wonderful mountains in the Snowmass area near Aspen. Others told tales of high adventure in Rocky Mountain National Park or the Sangre de Cristos. Such conversations were a wonderful way to fill the time away from the mountains we loved, and were as natural to us as political conversations in other places, with other people. There was a difference, however, between talk of the mountains, and talk of "The San Juans".

OPPOSITE: Cement Creek winds its way through the mountains between Silverton and Gladstone.

Dell A. McCoy Photograph

Dell A. McCoy Photograph

The town of Silverton, as viewed from the north, sits below Grand Turk mountain on the right. Storm clouds gather above Snowden Peak down the canyon to the south.

Although some of us had driven through them, none of my close friends had ever actually spent time in the San Juan backcountry. I found that this was true of a great many Coloradans. While many mountain lovers live in Colorado (people who hike extensively in the eastern and central mountains), relatively few of them ever get around to hiking in the San Juans. The reasons given are numerous. The San Juans are too distant from where we live. They hold great depths of snow which make hiking impossible until well into the summer. The trails are said to be unbelievably rugged, and access roads non-existent. These reasons, largely false, are not, I am convinced, the real reason for the failure of many to hike the San Juans. The reasons are spiritual. When one speaks in hushed tones, with awe, about a region, one secretly fears that the beauty he believes to reside there might prove more mundane in experience than imagination. The San Juans are a sacred place of the mind, a last remaining frontier.

The Magnificent San Juans

by Steven J. Meyers   141

For a person who values wildness and rugged beauty no disappointment could equal the loss of this frontier. I am happy to report that no such loss occurs with experience. As wonderful as the San Juans are in the mind, they are infinitely better in the flesh. Nine years of living in their heart has cost me none of my expectation. My awe remains intact.

I can still remember the first time I saw them. I was in graduate school, working on a thesis in landscape photography, and in the process of returning to Denver from a photographic trip to the canyonlands of southeast Utah. I had driven across the central mountains on my way to the desert, going through Grand Junction, and had decided to return through the San Juans. My route took me through Monticello, then Dove Creek and Mancos, to Durango skirting the range. From Durango the road climbed quickly up into the mountains, but I was so much *in* them I couldn't really *see* them. Besides, I was tired and smelly, hungry and needing a shave. My mind was not right for such a place. I continued on until I came to Molas Pass near Silverton. There the immediacy of the place overwhelmed my narrow preoccupations. I saw the jagged peaks of the Grenadier Range and the Needles spread out before me and knew some day I would have to return. A few years later I moved to Silverton.

Describing the San Juans is not an easy task. Even pinpointing their location proves difficult. They exist not as a single range, nor simple collection of ranges, and the boundaries which separate them from mountain regions of other names are in some cases indistinct. The first formal mapping of the region was done in the summer of 1874 by a group which included Allen D. Wilson, Franklin Rhoda and Fred Endlich. They, along with two packers and a "general assistant" ventured into the San Juans not altogether sure of what they would find. Perhaps Rhoda's initial description of the San Juans (made at the beginning of his report on their topography) best describes the region: "In describing a river or a simple range of mountains, the order of sequence is laid down in nature; all you have to do is commence at one end of the line and follow it. The mountains in the so-called San Juan country, however, are very complicated, and present no definite lines that may be followed in a description without leaving much untold. They appear, not in a single range, not in a succession of ranges, but as a great mass." That great mass, roughly seventy miles by one hundred miles in size, lies west of the San Luis Valley, east of the Great Basin ranges beginning with the La Sal mountains in Utah, south of a line connecting Montrose and Gunnison in Colorado, and north of the plateaus and mesas which lie along the Colorado-New Mexico border. There are places where the mountains bleed through this description, and where the high desert enters, but this is a good general description of their location.

If location and general features defy description, how should one approach their geology? The com-

plexity is overwhelming. Examples of volcanic and sedimentary rock exist, and in some places (the mountains surrounding Ouray, for example) the line of demarcation is clear. In other places mountains of clearly distinct geology rise up from a sea of surrounding complexity (the quartzite Grenadiers near Molas Pass are an example).

A simplified chronology of the region might be constructed as follows: Eighty to sixty-five million years ago much of the San Juan area was covered by water from what was then a much larger Gulf of Mexico. Around fifty million years ago uplifting raised the land above the water. Thirty-five million years ago volcanic activity began, and five million years later the weight of lava flows caused depressions to form, radically altering the topography. Twenty-eight million years ago volcanic activity increased dramatically and significant fracturing of the existing rock began. Once again, about twenty-six million years ago the accumulated lava forced the sinking of the surface and the formation of collapsed calderas. Twenty-five million years ago granites were injected into the fissures which remained from earlier cataclysm, and metal ores flowed as well. Finally, about ten-thousand years ago, heavy glaciation carved the existing topography into the horned peaks, hanging valleys, cirques and canyons which remain today.

This scenario covers much of the San Juan's mountain formation. It also hints at a factor which would prove significant in the area's commercial and social development: the presence of heavy mineralization. When Wilson and Rhoda and their companions ventured into the San Juans in the summer of 1874 they found an area of exquisite beauty and ruggedness. They also found that they had been preceded by prospectors and miners.

Lake City was in its early days up in the northern San Juans. A tentative settlement (Utes, unhappy about the arrival of settlers, frequently raided the site) was beginning in the south, near the present location of Durango. Smack in the middle of the mountain mass the pioneer survey party ran into a beehive of activity. Just below the divide on their journey west and south they came upon Howardsville and the early stages of development in Bakers Park, the area that would become Silverton. Major discoveries of gold and silver were made. Toll roads were built to facilitate access. Finally, railroads were built, threading their way into the heart of the district.

At one time the Denver and Rio Grande hauled ore out of the area, and provisions in, from both the north and the south. The Rio Grande Southern circled the San Juans from the south and west, and three separate railroads ran up from Silverton into the mining communities and mine sites surrounding Bakers Park.

The history of the region is inextricably linked with mining. When metal prices were good, the region flourished, when they were bad, it suffered. Many

Winter snow fills the Animas River canyon north of Silverton.

OVERLEAF: The San Juans rise above Trout Lake in the vicinity of Ophir. Water tank and railroad grade of the Rio Grande Southern are visible in the center of the photograph.

Dell A. McCoy Photograph

Steven J. Meyers Photograph

modern communities in the region have broadened their economic base in order to free themselves from the boom and bust cycle of the past. Lake City, which has a longer history of tourism than other San Juan towns, now finds itself deriving most of its income from this industry. Creede, once dominated by mining, and victim to its fortunes, now finds itself justly famous for the quality of its repertory theater. Telluride, until very recently predominantly a mining community, has recovered from its economic woes through the development of skiing and a world famous series of festivals. Silverton, for many years the center of intense mining activity, has found its fortunes more and more dependent on its tourist trade. Still, it remains unique in the San Juans. A fairly large community (by San Juan standards), with a continuous history of mining from the time of its inception, it continues to be home for working

miners and the businessmen who service them. Recent economic woes at its largest producing mine have created doubts about the future of mining in the San Juans, and many predict the ultimate demise of mining in the region. There are others, however, who remember the past, feel deeply connected with mining and the tradition it represents, and insist that Silverton will remain "the mining town that wouldn't quit".

Many of those towns that did quit are now present as reminders of the past, and sit, in various stages of disrepair and disintegration, among the mountains and along the jeep roads of the San Juans. They are called ghost towns. I have never encountered ghosts within them, only memories, and reveries about what had once been.

Thinking past the ghost towns, before the presence of man in the region, one confronts the

Somewhat isolated from the other peaks of the San Juans, Engineer Mountain sits astride the Cascade and Lime Creek drainages, midway between Durango and Silverton.

most significant frontier to be encountered in the San Juans, a frontier of attitude.

Our historic concept of frontier, our tales of mountains crossed and lands subdued, has its roots in the soil of human arrogance, in the belief that land can be conquered. If there is one especially important gift to be received from the San Juans, it is the knowledge that this is folly, that land may be damaged, but never conquered. In a small way we learn this when we get a sense of historical geology and geologic time. In a much more immediate way a place may impose this reality upon us. The mountains of the San Juans are such a place. In them it is possible to cross the boundary from our historic arrogance to a much more appropriate humility.

The heart of the San Juans, some of its most mountainous terrain lies within the boundaries of the Weminuche Wilderness, a 430,000 acre area of dense forest and delicate tundra, of roaring waterfalls and quiet streams, of lush meadows and jagged peaks. The area, which straddles the Continental Divide from the vicinity of Pagosa Springs in the east to near Silverton in the west, is the heart of the San Juans in more than just a geographic sense. Human presence in the wilderness is minimal. It is easy to imagine the world as it was before man emerged, and as it might be when we have gone. The raw beauty of the mountains helps put our humanity in perspective. It restores an appropriate sense of our place in the natural order. Such perspective is difficult to gain in civilized surroundings, but quite obvious here. This perception in no way diminishes our true importance as a part of nature but it does strip away a great deal of accumulated false pride. As wonderful as the living communities, ghost towns and history of the San Juans are, no trip to them is complete without a journey to their heart, the wilderness.

There is much in the San Juans to appeal to visitors, and interests of all kinds may be indulged here. For the motor traveler there are good roads through breathtaking terrain, with friendly towns interspersed at comfortable intervals. For the four-wheeler there is an abundance of jeep roads, many over high passes which allow access to the delicate and beautiful world of the high tundra. For the hiker there is an unbelievable wealth of roadless wilderness and primitive area. Historians find much remaining evidence of mining activity and narrow-gauge railroading, along with the towns which came and went during Colorado's mining heyday. Naturalists find an incredible variety of wildlife, including many of the large mammals (elk, mule deer, mountain sheep and goats, bear and others) which are becoming increasingly difficult to see in other places. Wildflower lovers find a profusion of color in the low meadows as well as the alpine environment. It is a landscape and nature photographer's dream. All of this is available without great mountaineering skills, or the courage of a lion. You don't have to be a mountain man or trapper to enjoy the San Juans.

If your taste runs toward adventure, however, there is probably as much opportunity here as anywhere. In the wilderness areas which are closer to population centers there is much beauty, but nothing equals, for me, the knowledge that I am out by myself far from the haunts of others. In the San Juans,

notably in the deeper recesses of the Weminuche, it is possible to spend a great deal of time alone, or at least apart from human company, for one is never alone in the wilderness. It is the knowledge of the existence of this remoteness from people which lends the San Juans their mystique, and to a certain extent it is justified.

There was a time when I would leave a backpack at the ready, with a sleeping bag, small shelter, some extra clothing, a lot of tea bags, dried soup and sugar by my door. Whenever an opportunity arrived it would find itself strapped to my back bouncing along a trail somewhere. Often I would see no one. Similarly, I once was able to spend a month fishing a favorite stream, every day, and during that month I never came across another fisherman. I am convinced that those days of hiking and fishing alone taught me more about myself and the world around me than years in towns, schools and other civilized places ever did. I am not anti-social; I am simply compelled to report what I experienced. I believe that those precious days might never have occurred had I been hiking or fishing somewhere else. The San Juans are, indeed, special.

For the European, trapped in a centuries old

Partially obscured by storm, Wilson Peak towers over the surrounding mesas west of Telluride.

The Emma Mine, one of several surviving structures in the Red Mountain mining district, sits below the Red Mountains near the top of Red Mountain Pass between Ouray and Silverton.

148

Just south of Ouray, Red Mountain Pass climbs out of the Uncompahgre Gorge. Mount Abrams (right) dominates the view looking south, while Grand Mesa appears on the northern horizon (below) looking north.

Dell A. McCoy Photograph

culture of class distinctions and traditions which have assumed the status of truth, for a religious radical or reformer, the dream of America was one of vastness, an intellectual vastness within which to experiment, and a physical vastness in which to do it. Arrival on the continent involved a great deal of hardship, but the land was incredibly rich and worthy of the enterprise. Virgin forests still towered over their carpeted floors. Vegetation and game flourished. As the settlers grew in numbers, the reformers and radicals found themselves outnumbered by people who, although more adventurous than those they left behind, carried with them the traditional values of their homelands. It mattered little. For the ones who would leave these values behind forever there remained the huge and never ending wilderness.

For nearly two-hundred years the explorers and trappers, the men who found little in cities to please

them, continued to move westward. Behind them followed settlement. The first waves of settlers were comprised of pioneers. After the pioneers came settlers more and more infused with the cultivated tastes they had inherited from their complex, but similar pasts. Along the way something uniquely American emerged: a glorification of adventure and the pioneering spirit, a belief that wilderness would always exist to challenge us, and a nearly religious belief in the purity and goodness of man's successful domination of nature. As long as something wild remained, there was a frontier to be conquered. That it has occurred, only recently, to the majority of adventurers that this attitude was ultimately self-defeating is testimony to the greatness of this former wilderness called North America. That we have stopped in time to save a few pockets of wilderness from extinction is a credit to our ability to learn. Or, perhaps not.

LEFT: The town of Ouray rests under fresh snow.

A popular eating establishment with an Old West atmosphere, The Bent Elbow on Blair Street in Silverton features hearty food and a honky tonk piano player.

It is possible that our notion of frontier (which once derived its strength from the attributes of the land which inspired it, then became perverted into a misguided notion of human triumph over nature, and now finds itself returning in its original form as an attitude of deep respect and awe) returns not because we have learned, but because the land itself was too strong to suffer the indignity forever.

When we confront one of these last barriers of the land's resistance we are capable of many responses. One is to simply fail to see the dimensions of the struggle. One is to believe that the battle can be won, that frontier and pioneer go hand in hand, that man and nature are adversaries. Another is to find yourself aligned with those who moved westward, not to conquer a territory, but simply to get away from the sadness of watching a virgin land being temporarily stripped of its dignity.

In the San Juans there is evidence of all aspects of this history of man's interaction with the land. There

remains land which is unscarred, land which inspires profound respect. There is evidence of the history of man's noblest aspiration, to live and prosper in harmony with a place. There is evidence of civilization in most of its forms and states of achievement, from pioneer spirit, to settlement, to decay. The perceptive might read these messages anywhere. Even ordinary people, like me, see them in a place like the San Juans.

Finally, when I contemplate just what it is that inspires my deep affection and profound respect for this place, it is as much my gratitude for what it has taught me as my awe in response to the magnitude of its reality, the details which comprise its existence. It is my belief that some of this will become a part of anyone who visits here.

Come to the San Juans to experience whatever you hope to experience. Their reality is, indeed, better than any vision of them, and an experience of them is not likely to leave you disappointed. Or unchanged.

151

ABOVE: Mount Sneffels and the Sneffels Range lie between Ouray and Telluride in the western San Juans.

The Trout Lake trestle near Ophir, one of the few remaining structures of the Rio Grande Southern.

Dell A. McCoy Photograph

Beautiful Lake San Cristobal in the northern San Juans is the lake from which Lake City received its name.

Aspen, Fortunes From

In the State of Colorado everything west of the "Front Range" cities—Ft. Collins, Denver, Colorado Springs, Pueblo, Trinidad—is mountains, contrasting sharply with the vast rolling plains to the east. Within this region, remarkable for its geographic variety, are 53 peaks towering more than 14,000 feet above the distant sea. Great rivers—Missouri, Arkansas, Rio Grande, Colorado—have their ultimate sources along the Continental Divide, which wriggles along a lofty route through Colorado from Wyoming to New Mexico. Only at those state boundaries does the great divide recede below 10,000 feet.

Almost in the exact center of that mountainous expanse lies Aspen, situated only a dozen miles west of the Continental Divide and barely 20 miles from Mt. Elbert, the state's highest summit at 14,443 feet. From northeast to southwest, Aspen is encircled by 14,000-footers—Holy Cross, Massive, Elbert, La Plata, Huron, Castle, Pyramid, South Maroon, North Maroon, Snowmass and Capitol. Only a mile away in almost any direction from the 7,800-foot confluence of the Roaring Fork River and Hunter, Castle and Maroon Creeks is the 10,000-foot topographic contour.

Not much more than a century ago the Roaring Fork valley was within the Ute Indian Reservation, and because this upper end was protected by a mountain wall, it was one of the last areas to be explored by those who sought gold and silver. In 1863 and again in 1868, Colorado's Territorial Governors (John Evans and Alexander Hunt) negotiated a treaty by which the upper portion of the Roaring Fork valley was placed just outside of the reservation. Although a few early trappers and adventurers had come close to Aspen's future site to the west and north, it seems that the first authenticated visit was that of Dr. F.V. Hayden in 1873 during his systematic survey of the Territory for the U.S. Government. His group assigned names to many geographic features in the course of their work.

Colorado became a state in 1876, and a year or so later some prospectors from Leadville crossed the Continental Divide at Independence Pass, which is now the highest (12,095 feet) highway crossing of the divide. In the summer of 1879 one small group, coming down the valley from Independence Pass, established Ute City, where Aspen now stands. They were joined by another group which had come from the south, over Taylor, Pearl or Coffee Pot Pass. Because of the Indian massacre of the Meeker family, Governor Frederick Pitkin advised the prospectors to leave the area; and, most of them did so, but returned in the spring of 1880. These early prospectors discovered silver-ore deposits in the steep hillsides all around Ute City, as well as the nearby communities of Independence and Highland. Of all these embryonic towns only Aspen (renamed in 1880) has survived.

The prospectors soon sold their claims to outsiders who could provide the capital and expertise to develop and operate the mines, and before 1880 was over Aspen's bonanza was known from coast to coast. Cincinnati investors, B. Clark Wheeler, Charles A. Hallam and David M. Hyman, were the principal figures behind Aspen's meteoric silver boom. Newcomers arrived by the hundreds during 1880. The townsite was laid out, a post office established, construction of the Clarendon Hotel begun; and road building commenced over Independence and Taylor Passes. The silver ore was taken out of the valley by pack-trains of mules, jackasses and burros, over Independence Pass, to the Denver & Rio Grande railroad at Granite, or to the smelters at Leadville. Other roads, meeting the D&RG at Buena Vista, surmounted Cottonwood or Tin Cup Passes to reach Taylor Park, whence the traverse over Taylor Pass provided access to Aspen. A road down the Roaring Fork to Glenwood Springs was built during 1881-1883.

The first big discovery occurred in the Aspen mine late in 1884, and before year-end 100 miners were extracting, every day, 100 tons of ore worth $10,000. Impassable during the winter months, the roads over Pearl, Taylor and Independence Passes became massive traffic jams as outbound ore wagons met those inbound laden with supplies, machinery and household goods. Aspen's known population soared beyond 5000, with perhaps as many uncounted. The nation's first hydro-electric plant was installed during 1887, while everyone awaited the arrival of railroad tracks which would link Aspen with the country's commercial centers. From its railhead at Rock Creek the D&RG extended its narrow-gauge track down the Eagle River, thence down the Grand River to Glenwood Springs, where it went up the Roaring Fork to Aspen. A work train reached the city before the end of October. Meanwhile, the Colorado Midland railroad (backed by the AT&SF railway system) had laid its rails westward from Leadville directly toward the Continental Divide, which was pierced by a 2160-foot-long tunnel whose apex attained the incredible altitude of 11,530 feet. The boring of the tunnel at such great elevation so delayed the Colorado Midland that its first train to reach Aspen (from Basalt on the Roaring Fork) did not arrive until early February of 1888. Although its route from Leadville to Aspen was considerably shorter than that of the D&RG (82 vs 132 miles), the

Silver And Snow

by Robert A. LeMassena

Colorado Midland's location was handicapped by very steep grades, severe curvature, and heavy snowfall.

Following the arrival of the railroads, Aspen's growth surged even greater. Sometimes 40 carloads of ore were shipped out in one day. The telephone line reached the city. Electrically powered streetcars were introduced. Two new hotels were built, as well as an opera house and brewery. The official population count for the county reached 8800 in 1890, the year in which Aspen had two newspapers. Other new buildings included the County Courthouse, the telephone exchange, the city hospital, and several churches. Wealth flowed from the mountains in a seemingly endless stream which astounded the entire country, particularly when a pure silver nugget, weighing almost a ton, was extracted from the Smuggler mine. But that magnificent era came to a sudden end after India's mints discontinued the purchase of silver for coinage. At the beginning of its productive period around Aspen, silver was worth $1.15 an ounce, dropping to 87c in 1892; ten years later it had sunk to only 53c. Aspen became a dying city, as mines and concentrators ceased production, and distant smelters were closed—forever. Some of the best mines continued sporadic production, but by 1925 the state's total production, worth just over 2-million dollars, was only 10% of what it had been in 1891.

As silver mining declined, agriculture and cattle raising became more important in the economy of the Roaring Fork valley, though not in Aspen itself because the city was surrounded by steep-sided mountains, a handicap which was to become the dominant factor in Aspen's renaissance. A 1925 D&RGW railroad timetable could say only that there was some fine hunting and fishing near Aspen; and a solitary mixed-train made a daily round-trip from Glenwood Springs. During the terrible business depression of the early-1930s Aspen's population sank below 1000, and houses could be bought for their long-unpaid taxes—about $1000, furnished.

At the beginning of the 1940-decade Aspen was so small that no one used telephone numbers; one merely asked the operator for Doc Twining, and she would call around until she found him. There was so little traffic on E. Main St. that unconcerned dogs slept in front of the Jerome Hotel. The hotel's Bamboo Bar was deserted, except when some ranchers dropped in to discuss water, cattle or hay. Any chance visitor was interviewed by the editor of the Aspen Times, so desperate was his need for copy. On one occasion the sheriff didn't bother to pursue a car thief who drove through town toward Independence Pass. "He'll come walking back

before too long. They haven't plowed off the snow beyond the National Forest boundary." All meals at the Jerome Hotel were 50c, and rooms were $2. The daily-except-Sunday noontime arrival of the "Daily Excitement", as the D&RGW's 2-car train from Glenwood Springs was called, was often the biggest event of the day. Although Walt Acheson could have carried the mail sack easily the two blocks from depot to post office, he was given a wartime

The Jerome Hotel, the Opera House, the Court House, and St. Mary's Church are easily discerned in this panorama of Aspen taken from Ruthie's Run on Aspen Mountain in 1955.

155

Robert A. LeMassena Photograph

Above Maroon Lake at nearly 10,000 feet, North and South Maroon Peaks soar to 14,014 and 14,156 feet into the pellucid blue sky.

OPPOSITE ABOVE: The attire and skis—and the visibility of the Jerome Hotel from the bottom of the big lift—date this scene to 1955. The ride to the top took a very cold 45 minutes; hence, the need for coats and robes.

OPPOSITE BELOW: Pyramid Peak (14,018 feet) separated East and West Maroon Creeks. Climbers found this mountain extremely dangerous because of its loose rock.

"T-card" for gasoline because he had injured his leg in a mining accident. Unable to use more than a fraction of his allotment, Walt would take sportsmen over precarious roads in his pickup truck into the high country, fortifying himself first with a couple of shots of Old Fitzgerald as a temerity deterrent. "I'd sure hate to drive on some of those roads when I was sober!" Freddie Fisher, a well-known big-band clarinet player, moved to Aspen "because it was the most remote spot that I could find." His euphoria didn't last very long, however, because somebody from the "outside world" discovered something which Aspenites had known for 60 years: SNOW.

Aspen's snow was light and dry, like powder, and it lay on shaded north-facing slopes until well beyond the equinox. Skiers found Aspen's slopes a paradise, so different from those of other areas in the USA or Europe, where the snow was heavy, moist or icy. Skiers told other skiers, and before long a chair-lift had been installed to the top of Aspen Mountain at 9700 feet. In time, it was extended to the summit of Ajax Mountain (11,500 ft.), providing skiers with a 4-mile run with about 4000 feet of vertical descent. Aspen's fabulous snow attracted skiers from everywhere, and even long-vacant stores and storerooms were hastily converted to bunkhouses, where a dozen strangers might occupy a single room, with community washrooms located down-the-hall or even next-door somewhere. Skis were not allowed inside the buildings, and boots were deposited in entryways.

Summertime tourists also discovered Aspen, and the 2-lane road from Glenwood Springs became a 4-lane freeway. Other ski areas, at Highlands and Snowmass, were established, and summertime

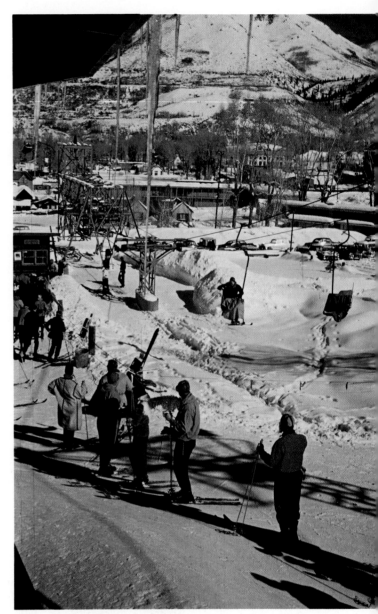

Robert A. LeMassena Photograph

Robert A. LeMassena Photograph

resorts sprang up all over the upper end of the Roaring Fork valley. Aspen became a center of artistic and philosophical culture; gourmet restaurants catered to more sophisticated palates; wealthy people built magnificent homes on the hillsides overlooking the slopes and meadows. Once the habitat of "ski-bums", who worked at anything to indulge their sport, and weekenders, who could afford only minimal lodging, Aspen metamorphosed into playground for the affluent, who arrived by private jet-aircraft from around the world.

In the mid-1980s Aspen appears to be in the midst of a cultural and recreational boom which resembles the frantic mining explosion just a century ago. No one knew then how it would end, and likewise no one knows today what might lie ahead for Aspen.

157

$\mathcal{M}$any of Colorado's trails among the columbine were actually steel. Much of the legend and lore of early Colorado rode on the tracks of narrow-gauge steam trains. The Colorado Railroad Museum has preserved the mystique of the Rocky Mountain slim-gauge for future generations.

The museum, located in Golden, Colorado since 1958, has the most extensive collection of railroad equipment in the Rocky Mountain region. The collection has grown from meager beginnings to include examples of standard gauge, traction, cog, and the largest inventory of Colorado narrow-gauge assembled at one location.

The main building, built to resemble a typical railway station, houses two floors of memorabilia from all eras of the state's rail history. Within its walls can be found many treasures. One of the few examples of Otto Mears' silver filigree railroad passes may be seen. Many original letters and telegrams describe both the amusing and tragic events that occurred during the state's fascinating rail history. Many original photographs by William H. Jackson depicting life in the late 1800s line the walls.

Families may explore the grounds and discover forty pieces of narrow-gauge and twenty assorted pieces of standard-gauge equipment. Motive power includes nine steam engines, two diesels, and three

The Colorado

trolleys. Of special interest are three "Galloping Geese" from the Rio Grande Southern. These were homemade railcars built by the railroad to economize its operations. Built from Pierce Arrow automobile parts and a lot of mechanical ingenuity, these creations are one of the most unique examples of rail transportation in the west.

One-hundred year old plus Denver & Rio Grande Western #346 is the oldest operating locomotive in the state. On certain weekends throughout the year volunteer crews steam up the engine and operate it over the museum's trackage. Visitors may catch a ride and relive the thrills of steam travel.

In 1984 the museum acquired an extensive narrow-gauge collection from the Durango area. This acquisition of rolling stock and related rail paraphernalia greatly enhances the museum's collection.

The museum is located just east of Golden at the foot of North Table Mountain. It is easily reached from Interstate 70 west of Denver. At exit 265 go west to McIntyre Road, then north to 44th Ave. and then west again to the Colorado Railroad Museum.

OPPOSITE: One of only 8 Baldwin locomotives constructed by Baldwin for the DSP&P railroad, No. 191 is Colorado's oldest locomotive, having been built in January 1880. It has been restored, and is now on exhibit at the Colorado Railroad Museum in Golden.

No. 2 Motor, with Pierce-Arrow body, ran for many years on the Rio Grande Southern before coming to the Colorado Railroad Musuem, where it is operated on occasion.

Jim Wild Photograph

Railroad Museum

by Jim Wild and Dwayne Easterling

Colorado's 2nd-oldest locomotive, built by Baldwin in July 1881 for the D&RG railway, is also at the Colorado Railroad Museum, and it is operated several times each year.

4

Piu lento

rit.

pur - ple robed West, the land that is best, The
nymphs of the grove in their lone - li - ness rove, But the
fair West - ern home, may the col - um - bine bloom Till our

pi - o - neer land that we love._____
col - um - bine blooms just the same._____
great moun - tain riv - ers run dry._____

CHORUS a tempo   accel.   accel.

'Tis the land where the col-um-bines grow,___ O-ver-look-ing the plains far be-low,___ While the

rit.

cool sum-mer breeze in the ev-er-green trees Soft-ly sings where the colum-bines grow.___

Where The C. G. 4